A Wrestling Life

A Wrestling Life 2

More Inspiring Stories of Dan Gable

DAN GABLE

with KYLE KLINGMAN

UNIVERSITY OF IOWA PRESS *Iowa City*

University of Iowa Press, Iowa City 52242
Copyright © 2017 by the University of Iowa Press
www.uipress.uiowa.edu
Printed in the United States of America

Design by Richard Hendel

The University of Iowa Press is a member of Green Press Initiative
and is committed to preserving natural resources.

Printed on acid-free paper

Library of Congress Cataloging-in-Publication Data
Names: Gable, Dan, author. | Klingman, Kyle, collaborator.
Title: A wrestling life : 2 : more inspiring stories of Dan Gable /
Dan Gable, with Kyle Klingman.
Description: Iowa City : University of Iowa Press, [2017] | Includes index.
Identifiers: LCCN 2016042841 | ISBN 978-1-60938-484-5 (cloth) |
ISBN 978-1-60938-587-3 (pbk) | ISBN 978-1-60938-485-2 (ebk)
Subjects: LCSH: Gable, Dan. | Wrestling coaches—United States—
Biography. | Iowa Hawkeyes (Wrestling team)—Anecdotes.
Classification: LCC GV1196.G33 A3 2017 | DDC 796.812—dc23
LC record available at https://lccn.loc.gov/2016042841

CONTENTS

THANKS!

I've found that when one spends valuable time on anything, it tends to come back in rewarding waves. My first book, *A Wrestling Life*, has done exactly that.

In the final moments of the 2012 Olympic wrestling trials in Iowa City, sports writer Scott Schulte approached me about an article he wanted to do on my late family and sister, Diane. I agreed, thinking that it was just a possibility and would not actually come to pass. Yet, Scott followed up quickly with a first draft based on our conversation, and then again with a completed article.

It was good work, and my wife, Kathy, was impressed. So when Scott went another step and asked about potentially doing a book, he already had the good ear of my wife, which made it a real possibility. Then chapters started flowing in after our interviews. With the help of the University of Iowa Press staff, Susan Hill Newton, Allison Means, Jim McCoy, Elisabeth Chretien, and Karen Copp, it became a reality.

So now I'm here again, and with a second book!

Because of the valuable time spent on the first book, my wife and I experienced something that never would have happened otherwise. In my first book, Kathy talked about our wedding plans and how we had to change the date because of a wrestling event, and with that we lost the reception location and the band that we really wanted.

When *A Wrestling Life* came out in 2015, our daughters read this story for the first time. Not long after, the girls and their husbands told Kathy and me to save a particular date. The day of, we traveled about thirty miles out to the middle of nowhere to Fireside Winery near the Amana Colonies. It turned out that the girls were giving us the event we missed out on forty-one years earlier. Playing that night was the band we had wanted for our wedding reception, Milk and Honey, who were still together all these years later, though with a few alterations. So now we got to celebrate with and dance to this band after all. It was a pretty emotional evening for both of us.

That was quite a surprise for us, but there were more rewarding lessons for our family that came out of the experience of writing that book. I included a chapter on each of my four daughters, and each chapter gave me new insight into my family.

The chapter on my oldest daughter, Jenni, made me realize how special she felt being with her father. I always just took it for granted, but not anymore.

The chapter on Annie, the next in line, brought out just how special the Hawkeye wrestling program has always been to her. I never realized that before working on the book.

In Molly's chapter, I wrote about how she collapsed and passed out during an 800-meter relay race. I always found that so inspiring, that she was so driven and pushed herself so hard that she collapsed. For years that had been my goal in daily practices: to push myself so hard that I passed out. It never happened, even though a couple of times I may have been close. After working on this chapter though, I was reminded of the 1996 Olympics and one of Tom Brands's tough pre-final matches. Tom won, but I woke up in the trainer's room after passing out. So I actually did achieve that goal, just not in the way I always hoped.

The chapter on Mackie, my youngest, was the hardest to work on, but it proved to be very valuable in our relationship. It helped us understand each other in a way we never had before. I titled that chapter "Finishing Strong," which is quite appropriate, for it solved a lot of long-standing issues between us. The mystery was no longer a mystery, and our relationship has continued to improve since then. Without the book and that chapter, this might not have happened.

Of course, I owe so many thank-yous to so many people that this book could be just that: a book of thank-yous! I will mention an important one involving building performance, because it has helped so many people over the years.

When I arrived in Iowa City in the fall of 1972, one of Gary Kurdelmeier's visions was to start and fund a nonprofit wrestling club, the Hawkeye Wrestling Club, to build upon the excellence of the college wrestling program. Building up and improving the college program were going to take a lot of resources, and starting an outside club from scratch would take even more. We had strict orders from athletic administration to do this within NCAA rules. Plus, all funding had to be new money: taking only above current donations. This could have become a serious problem with athletic fundraisers, who were skeptical. The solution was Roy Carver: he decided to solely fund the Hawkeye Wrestling Club (HWC) above and beyond his normal contributions to the University of Iowa.

This arrangement worked well, and the club was formed and flourished. Then one day, years later, a call came in informing us that Roy had passed away from a heart attack during one of his many travels. By this time, I was the head wrestling coach of the program. Both Iowa and the club were doing extremely well.

The HWC had a budget, but Roy was paying it. Now, the club's sole source of funding was no longer there. I was starting to panic until a call came in from an interested fan named Herb Tyler who lived in Davenport, asking about the HWC and its funding. Herb had heard about our dilemma, and he happily wrote a considerable check to keep the HWC budget alive until we could find a long-term funding solution. Without that initial check, things could have gone downhill quickly for the HWC. Word of our funding situation got out, and the club quickly went from having one donor to one hundred donors. The strict rules of contributions to the University of Iowa stayed in place as well. Thankfully, we had a much bigger base of wrestling fans at this point, compared to our start just a few years back. There was quite a difference between just starting out in building an organization for performance, having the organization and the performance built, and now just solving problems.

The Carver family and its trust continue their help with wrestling, athletics, and the University of Iowa hospitals. The Herb Tyler family is the same, and to the thousands of current donors, many thanks. To all the members of the HWC and the Hawkeye Area Wrestling Klub (HAWK), the same thanks. It all started with Gary Kurdelmeier, and it led to many others, like the Ed McGinness family and the Tom Senneff family of the University of Iowa College of Law, who kept us honest. It continues today with many who contribute for the fun and excitement.

Today, there are more wrestling sponsors than ever, like the current granGABLE bike ride, headed by Josh Schamberger, president of the Iowa City/Coralville Area Convention & Visitors Bureau, Matt Phippen of Scheels, and the Iowa Bicycle Coalition, along with the cooperation of the University of Iowa Athletics Department, who are critical for continuing performance. Events like the granGABLE bike ride bring together folks who were around at different times, yet I don't get to see them often. One who was there from the start is Dave Culver, team manager back in the day. He is still there on each bike ride. Events like this always work both ways: they are good for the organizations and good for the participants. I wouldn't expect it any other way.

Another shout-out goes to a former walk-on wrestler of mine, Pablo Ubasa. He has joined forces with another great Iowa wrestling follower, my good friend Bob Altmaier. In Florida, I also have to give thanks for the support from Paul Thein, Ron Jones, and Vic Lorenzano.

Thanks to "the neighborhood" of Gary Kurdelmeier. Of course, to the many who came, picked up, and continue to carry the lessons with them as well as sharing them, like Lanny Davidson, John Degl, and Eric Koble—that's great! I absolutely love the leadership principle of affecting the masses in positive ways. Jody Strittmatter and Eric Juergens are doing so with their coaching of the Young Guns!

Congrats to Mike Finn (*WIN* magazine), named Top Wrestling Writer of 2016 by *Amateur Wrestling News* (Bob Dellinger award) and to Bryan Van Kley. My appreciation also goes out toward all the writers, journalists, media personalities, and event promoters who have written about both me and the sport of wrestling, starting with Russ Smith, Burke and Kevin Evans, Buck Turnbull, Dan McCool, Lanny Bryant, Ron Good, the Hoke family, and carries forward with Jim Nelson, Andy Hamilton, Martin Floreani, Marc Hansen, Gary Abbott, Mike Chapman, and many others.

Special thanks to Trip Hedrick of Championship Productions, Ted Miller of Human Kinetics, Nick Gallo and Neil Duncan of ASICS, Mike Allen, Jim Eash, and Wyatt Schultz for their lifelong contributions to the sport.

Many thanks to my coauthor, Kyle Klingman, for helping shape this read. Kyle, development director Mike Doughty, and local businessman Bob Buckley are in the middle of reshaping the look of the museum. Thanks to Warren DePrenger, Richard Small, Jed Brown, Chris McGowan, Melissa Wilkens, Jay Roberts (RIP), Bill Tragos, Gerald Brisco, Troy Peterson, Bill Murdock, Charlie Thesz, Paul Stinson, Jason Sanderson, Van Miller (RIP), Jerry Roling, Marti Roling, Lee Roy Smith, Brad Roling, Amy Roling, Greg Stockdale, Josh Whitinger, Jason Whitinger, Jarvis Whitinger, Ed Gallegos, Bill Roths, John Rigler, Tom Slowey, John Harris, Steve Silver, Terry Shockley, Sandy Shockley, Tom Penaluna, Dave Mills, Rick Young, Alan Rice, Glen Brand, Jim Brown, Jason Bodensteiner, Charlotte Bailey, and many other people and trusts for their contributions to the museum.

Gable Trained: An Introduction

In all my coaching and writing and speaking, I've always tried to convey good, useful messages that can help people not just be more effective wrestlers or professionals, but also live better lives. People have used the label "Gable Trained" (GT) over the years as a way of talking about the physical and mental training my wrestlers went through in order to become champions. I like the label, but I want it to mean more than that.

I've been able to have a very successful and productive life for the most part. When it's not as healthy, it also has turned around and become good again, and even better. The GT principles are the words that get the credit. Of course, lots of discipline and commitment hold these words in place!

It's almost like in life you can have lots of luck, but I, and we, know better. These fortunate achievements are determined ahead of time through extraordinary actions and knowledge. Throughout this book, Gable Trained principles will present themselves in subtle and not-so-subtle ways. Watch for them. And watch for them in your own life.

Born into a family of four (including myself), I was surrounded with *mentors* who guided me in great directions as a kid. Life was not complicated; in fact, it was *simple,* and the great *communication* was full time, including my spiritual directions. If my *focus* was off track, there were *consequences* that put me back in line. Everywhere around me, I saw good *examples* of what was good and I saw people working together, *teamwork*. Not many creations are perfect, so *adversity* pops up and needs to be handled, and for that to happen, *improvements* must be made. The memories—*remembering*—must stick with you to help your mission of the future. Knowing how to solidly build a good culture that lasts is determined by your roadmap of following a good plan, which results in precise *peaking*. Understanding your skill ability and conquering the skills of the trade help your *talent* level rise for great performances. The *excellence* that happens because of this knowledge will rise at each higher level because of your commitment to separate yourself from the pack. One always can use good *help*, so be open to it.

With all this comes a lot of good things because you are *preventing* the bad things. Even with preparation and *prevention*, crazy things happen sometimes. Eliminating those negative *unknowns* is best, and they will be scarce when you are prepared.

When good things happen, being *appreciative* is a reward for you and the person getting the appreciation. The different *tools* available to help performance are out there, and knowing which ones are best in each case is crucial. A good way to know that is to stay *current* on all that is important. This can be difficult, but for you achievers, that's just *normal* and way beyond others. With all this come the gains and the *victories*. Of course, going to battle ready and prepared will be determined by your ability to rely on your *recovery* methods. And for those who need or want to change for the better—don't procrastinate, for *The Longer, the Longer*.

MENTORS

There have been many people and groups who have provided guidance for my journey in faith, in family, and in wrestling. The more positive influences you can have early in life, the better you will be later in life. My earliest influences were my parents, the leaders at the Y, my eighth-grade Algebra teacher and wrestling coach Martin Lundvall, my high school wrestling coach Bob Siddens, my college wrestling coach Harold Nichols, my World team wrestling coach Doug Blubaugh, my Olympic wrestling coach Bill Farrell, and my first main professional boss Gary Kurdelmeier. But one doesn't outgrow needing good mentors. Organizations like the National Wrestling Coaches Association, USA Wrestling, and the National Wrestling Hall of Fame have provided critical leadership at critical times. I've had hundreds of mentors who have guided me when making difficult decisions and for spiritual leadership.

SIMPLICITY

Often a leader knows a lot, but leaders need to make sure that the people who are doing the work to be accomplished also know what they know. The easiest way to spread knowledge and make sure everyone is on the same page is to keep it simple.

COMMUNICATION

In any team, having good communication is vital. This goes both ways, from leader to team members, and from team members to leader. This is true in all aspects of life. In my first book, I wrote about almost losing Barry Davis from the Iowa wrestling team when he went missing right before the 1982 Big Ten wrestling tournament. He was worried that he couldn't make weight, so he went into hiding. I immediately put a plan in place that allowed me to find Davis at a grocery store. Barry Davis might not have become a three-time NCAA champion and an Olympic silver medalist had I not had an exceptional line of communication with my staff and with my athletes. They were the ones who helped me connect the dots. But I would not have had to do that if Barry had been more open with me before that. As I said, communication is as simple as a two-way street.

FOCUS

Having tunnel vision can be a good thing when it keeps you focused on a goal. I lost the 1970 NCAA tournament finals to Larry Owings because I allowed myself to be distracted by too many things: Owings's boast that he was going to beat me, the media attention, the honors and awards I was already receiving. I lost that tunnel vision, and so I lost that match. Owings had what I didn't have in that match: tunnel vision and focus. But after that loss is when I got really good. I recommitted myself to training at the highest possible level and went on to win the 1972 Olympics without surrendering a point. This only happened because I had tunnel vision.

CONSEQUENCES

There need to be consequences for unacceptable actions. This is true in any area of your life. The Iowa wrestling team won nine NCAA titles from 1978 through 1986—but we placed second to Iowa State in 1987. Why? Even though we were still winning on the mat, we didn't have the correct attitude and work ethic in and out of practice, and consequently, our focus was skewed. There was too much celebrating and not enough focus and hard work. And most important, there weren't consequences for these unacceptable actions and attitudes. It took four years for us to return to the top, and we were able to do it because the wrestlers were held more accountable. Even with acceptable actions, there can be consequences.

EXAMPLES

Without an example to work from, no one really knows what he or she is looking for. Actions are worth more than words. Implementing actions with your words is an ideal way to get your point across—and you need to do that daily.

TEAMWORK

Teamwork is important, no matter who you are and what you do. In athletics, in your family, or in your profession, teamwork is vital both to achieve great things and also to provide a support system. Good leaders bring together all the talent available and turn it into good results and meaningful victories. Most of the people I write about in my books were part of a larger winning formula. Teamwork starts at the top and works its way down. It takes every person understanding the mission, believing in it, and contributing to it for success to happen. In wrestling, there are individual champions, but by coming together, individual champions can win team championships. Never be too caught up in your own success to forget the teamwork that got you there, or that you are contributing to a larger goal. When you work together, you win together!

ADVERSITY

It is important to learn from adversity, but don't let it repeat itself. Take on adversity, but better yet, prevent it. The death of my sister, Diane, at the age of nineteen altered the course of my life. Had I understood some things better, I may have been able to prevent her murder. Within an hour of knowing of her death, I told my parents the name of the suspect. This information could have been known earlier. I don't dwell on this though. I learned some important lessons and moved forward with my life. I did what I felt I had to do to keep my remaining family together, and I looked at this adversity through Diane's eyes. I categorize adversity in two ways: life and death, and wins and losses.

IMPROVING

After a loss or a less-than-desirable outcome, focusing on turning the tables can be a great motivator. Don't focus on a loss or a lesser outcome! I have seen plenty of examples of this working for people throughout my career. In my first book, I wrote about a time in college when I placed two newspaper clippings in my wallet: one for motivation and the other to build confidence. The clipping for motivation included a quote from Marty Willigan of Hofstra University, who said he could beat me after I beat him 12–1. Focusing on payback for our match drove Willigan that season. I focused on improving that entire season. In the end, I proved Willigan wrong by pinning him in the 1969 NCAA tournament finals. But the same thing drove us both all season: to work harder and get better! Had the focus been one-sided, his chances of beating me would have been better.

REMEMBERING

Don't dwell on losses or setbacks, but don't forget the pain they cause. If there is no pain, you need to invest more in what you are doing. Mark these losses or setbacks down, and use them as motivation for future victories. Learn from your losses. I wrote about my loss to Larry Owings in my final match of my college career. I didn't dwell on that loss for long, but I remembered it, and I used it for future successes. After that loss, I learned more about my wrestling and about myself. I realized that I needed to work both smarter *and* harder than the other guy. I've always said that I won 181 matches, lost one, and then got good. Years later, when I was the head wrestling coach at Iowa, we had the chance to win ten NCAA championships in a row, but our streak stopped at nine. I marked that loss down and learned from it. We came back a few years later more disciplined and with better attitudes to dominate once again.

PEAKING

Stay focused and peak correctly. I lost my last match in college because I was focused on beating Mike Grant, the NCAA champion at the weight class above me, from the University of Oklahoma. I faced him and won that match six weeks before the NCAAs. Because he was my focus all year, I peaked at the wrong time. If I had focused on the NCAAs, as I should have, I would have peaked at a better time in order to win. With proper peaking, the likeliness of both wins—Grant and Owings—would have been much higher.

TALENT

Hard work and smart work take a person a long way, but witnessing and experiencing real talent make one feel the reality of perfection. Practice makes perfect, but a practice with talent brings one closer to perfection.

EXCELLENCE

Each level of competition needs a higher, smarter, and tougher level of commitment. If you keep working at the same level you did at a lower level of competition, you might not be as successful at higher levels. When you take a step up, you need to step up everything: your attitude, focus, work ethic, and dedication. This is true both in wrestling and in life. In this book, I describe how, whenever I reached the next level of competition, I had to step up everything I did. I trained more and trained harder in college than I did in high school. That level of dedication and focus went up again when I was training for the Olympics. Winning at the highest level is demanding. That separation from your previous level will be the difference.

HELP

Don't be afraid to accept help when you need it. Rick Sanders, our first US World champion in 1969, was a friend of mine on the 1972 Olympic team. He had won a silver medal at the 1968 Olympics, and in 1972 he knew he needed an extra edge to get past the Japanese wrestler. When he finished second again, he asked for my help in training. Sanders saw that my disciplined training methods had paid off with dominant performances the past couple years, and he wanted my help to train for the 1976 Olympics. Rick also saw the great performances of the Peterson brothers and others who trained with me. Unfortunately, Sanders died shortly after the 1972 Olympics in an automobile accident, and he didn't get the help he wanted.

PREVENTION

Prevention is the best way to prevent injury, ill health, mistakes on the mat, in one's profession, and in one's family life. In wrestling, I focus on prevention by being prepared on the mat and by making sure to properly cool down and spend time recovering. In my professional career, reviewing past mistakes and careful planning can prevent further mistakes. In family life, one needs to address problems or tensions so you can prevent small problems from turning into big problems. I believe that prevention is the most important tool anyone can use to achieve great things!

UNKNOWNS

You can't control everything, but you can control a lot. Keep the unknowns to a minimum. You should be completely confident with what you can do and should have very few question marks. Have backup plans for any question marks you may have.

APPRECIATION

Focus on what you have, not what you don't have. World-renowned author John Irving helped me understand how fortunate I am by writing insightful articles about my career. Seeing myself through his eyes made me look around at what I had—my family, my profession, and my victories—and really appreciate it in a new way. This kind of self-reflection and the insight of others can be a useful tool for gratitude.

In my first book, I discussed when I dropped down to the 112-pound weight class in high school to make way for my friend Marty Dickey at 120 pounds. Marty had always helped me with basic skills in life outside of wrestling, and I appreciated that. Marty's returned appreciation continued through his three sons, who all wrestled for Iowa.

TOOLS

When trying to achieve something, use all the tools you can. I used deductive reasoning and as many members of the team and staff as I could to find Barry Davis when he went missing during his sophomore year of college. Or look at how Gary Kurdelmeier worked every angle he could to get me to come to the University of Iowa as an assistant coach. In both cases, Kurdelmeier and I both used many of the tools at our disposal to effect positive change in someone else's life. Tools can be simple, special pieces of equipment or they can even be the people around you.

CURRENT

Every moment counts, and you can never afford to fall behind. Once when I wrestled at the Tbilisi tournament, I fell behind in points and the Soviets stopped the match so their athlete could win, even though there was plenty of time left on the clock for me to come back. In "The Gable Edge" chapter I'll show how I stayed current in the wrestling world as an athlete, coach, and promoter of the sport. No matter what you do in your profession, it is important to stay current. It is a daily process that never ends. You're constantly in a state of becoming.

NORMAL

Being normal and working just as hard as everyone else won't lead to great achievements. To achieve greatness, *your* "normal" should be above and beyond everyone else's normal. When I was training for wrestling, or coaching, I didn't work an eight-to-five job and then just go home. I worked from early in the morning to late at night, seven days a week, though I still made sure I took the time to recover properly. What was normal for me went above and beyond what other people considered normal. Never be satisfied with other people's normal!

VICTORY

There can be many different kinds of victory, and all of them are important. Most people think of victory as just defeating an opponent. But a victory can also be a new accomplishment or raising your own level of performance. It can be meeting a difficult goal or overcoming a difficult situation. Never overlook these kinds of victories, because they are important and can help drive and fuel further victories. I have written about how my daughter Molly did something I never accomplished in all my years of training and competing: she pushed herself so hard that she passed out during an 800-meter race. She didn't finish the race, but she still won a great victory. I am prouder of her for that than I would have been if she had finished and won the race.

RECOVERY

The ability to wake up daily and be ready to go depends on one's ability to energize his or her mind and body. Taking the time to fulfill these needs every day will take extreme discipline, yet it is the only way to maximize performance. Examples of ways to recover are the sauna, hot and cold plunges, showering, massages, sleeping, proper nutrition, doing your homework, spending time on the computer, watching television, listening to music, casual reading, hanging out with friends, going to work, spending time with family, and even indulging in vices in small doses—as long as the vices are legal and used as rewards.

THE LONGER, THE LONGER

The longer you let a problem go, the longer it takes to get back on track. In this book, I talk a lot about how the Hawkeyes failed to win their tenth consecutive NCAA championship because our discipline was not where it should have been. This problem took years to develop, and so we couldn't fix it overnight. It took us four years to get the right kind of attitude and work ethic back to the point where we won the national championship again. This principle works on the positive side of things, too. The longer you build a relationship the right way, the better chance it has to become a long-term success.

Puzzling

In order to make great teams, a coach needs to be able to fit many different pieces together, pieces that may not normally fit together in any other way. These different pieces may not always come together all the time, but getting them to match up at the proper time can make all the difference.

At my high school, West Waterloo, assembling the pieces of the wrestling puzzle started well before my coach, Bob Siddens, came on the scene. Because of this, he wasn't starting from scratch and, therefore, it was easier for Bob to put the pieces together.

Laying a foundation is always tough. West Waterloo had five straight state championships between 1942 and 1946 with coaches Finn Erikson (1942–43) and Roy Jarrard (1944–46). With this foundation, Coach Siddens reeled in eleven state championships from 1951 through 1977, as well as several second- and third-place team trophies over those years. Many of these great wrestlers graduated and moved on to championship college teams, and they helped to develop and support the total sport.

One such college was Cornell College in Mount Vernon, Iowa, which won the 1947 NCAA tournament with several West Waterloo wrestlers. *The Dream Team of 1947* by Arno Niemand tells the fascinating story of this historic season. In 1950, Siddens was himself a member of the NCAA championship team for Iowa State Teachers College, now the University of Northern Iowa, in Cedar Falls. It's unbelievable the effects these experiences have on a person—they carry them for life.

Even today, many different people continue to contribute to the sport, whether they're a former wrestler themselves or a family member or a friend of a wrestler. A great example is Dave Bunning, whose dad, Jim, was a state champion at West Waterloo in 1956. Dave contributes to the sport of wrestling at a high level. It's a system that carries on throughout families and through people's lifetimes. Look at me: I was a West Waterloo wrestling graduate and was positively affected by Coach Siddens; then I in turn helped positively affect Iowa State, the University of Iowa, USA wrestling, and the world of wrestling to this day.

Another great example is two-time West Waterloo state champion and two-time NCAA champion Dale Anderson and his contribution to Michigan State University and its wrestling program, as well as the Big Ten. In 1967, Michigan State won the NCAA wrestling team championship, being the first to do it from the Big Ten Conference. Dale brought with him West Waterloo's wrestling tradition and Bob Siddens's winning ways to help with that 1967 NCAA wrestling title. You can read about it in Dale Anderson's book on their performance, *A Spartan Journey*.

Back in the day, I watched Siddens take individuals from both sides of the tracks, get a lot out of them individually, and help them win as a team. He brought them together by helping them experience the individual excellence one needs in life to be successful in their professions and with their families. When all or even most of the wrestlers were able to do this at the same time, while working toward the same goal, it brought them together as a team in a way nothing else could.

One thing I've always liked about wrestling is that one wrestler can make a name for themselves, and it affects a whole town, state, or country. When an entire team can have this kind of success, it brings people together even more.

Bob Siddens would get the different kids to feed off each other, yet those weren't the only kinds of pieces that came together. Kids with a less-than-perfect home life, especially ones who might not have strong parental role models, often became more driven toward wrestling success and community involvement. Sometimes it was the families who were looking for something of value for their kids. They would see our wrestling team's success, both on the mat and in the community, and think, "I want my kid to go out for wrestling, because I know he will benefit." That was the thing: Coach Siddens led us so that *everyone* benefited: the wrestlers, the families, the school, and the community. And he was able to do this by bringing together all of these different pieces of the puzzle and by making them fit together in the right way at the right time. An interesting read about Bob is called *Siddens!*, authored by Don Huff and Mike Chapman. That book gives more insight into Bob's career.

Another good example of puzzling pieces together occurred between me and Chuck Jean of Albert Lea, Minnesota. He and I were two pieces of a puzzle who would not normally fit together. Chuck was always very social, while I was more quiet and a home-body. Without wrestling, we probably would not have gotten along. Through wrestling, we fit together as part of the larger puzzle that made Iowa State wrestling.

Chuck was a year behind me in school, which was probably a good thing for me. The rule of not competing for the school as fresh-men was good for many, as it gave us time to adjust to the level of discipline needed for competition at this level, as well as the aca-demic expectations, but it was not good for Chuck. Without com-petition as his main focus, Chuck jumped right into the social scene of college, and that became his top priority. Luckily, by the time he came along, I was already set in my ways in terms of practicing, working out, and studying.

In spite of our different temperaments, Chuck and I got along well. There's just something about Chuck that made you like him, and he definitely made a name for himself, both in the wrestling world and in the social world on campus.

Chuck liked to work out late at night when the ISU training facilities were closed. At some point, he discovered that the underground steam tunnels on campus were a good place to run during the cold Iowa winter nights. The tunnels went all over campus and were filled with heated pipes, so the temperature was well over one hundred degrees, which was great for when he needed to lose a few extra pounds for weigh-ins before a match.

One night he asked me to join him on a run through the steam tunnels. I had never been down in them and was curious, so I agreed. We set out late at night and ran to the nearest manhole cover on campus. Chuck slid it open, we climbed down, and then he put the cover back on. We were in a dark tunnel that was hot and steamy. Chuck's flashlight showed me what we were up against: pipes were everywhere, a few of them low hanging, and even some rats here and there. It was hot and dangerous, especially when running. The flashlight helped, but it was too dangerous to run fast. But wow did I sweat!

At some point not long into our run, I asked, "How do you know where you are?" I trusted Chuck, and wasn't too worried about getting lost in the maze of tunnels, but wondered about how he navigated them.

Chuck responded, "You don't. Not to worry though, because there are many manholes for escaping."

Chuck wasn't one to train too long, so shortly after that we stopped and went up to what I thought would be civilization. This particular manhole cover was right in the middle of campus, and we came up in the middle of a protest against the Vietnam War that was just quieting down for the night. Many of the student protesters had just laid down in their sleeping bags to spend the night outside so they could continue their protest first thing in the morning.

Needless to say, we surprised several of them, coming up out of the ground right beside them! At this point, I just wanted to run back to the house, but Chuck apparently didn't agree with this group. He picked up a few of the sleeping bags and shook them so the students slid right out! I grabbed him and started running. Chuck came along with me but was grumbling to himself the whole way. I don't think he wanted to be done with that group just yet.

Anyway, I thought that was the end of it. Apparently the students at the protest weren't happy about Chuck's actions though. None of the protesters recognized him, so he didn't get in trouble, but they did recognize me. I got called into the vice president's office shortly afterward, and the administration put a letter of censure into my file. Any more trouble, and there could be serious consequences for me.

So my one time in the steam tunnels under ISU was over. It made no sense to me as a training method, but it did to Chuck. It must have worked for him, too, because he won two NCAA titles at Iowa State. He had to transfer shortly after his second title, and went on to win two more national titles in the NAIA division for Adams State University in Alamosa, Colorado. Those last two were mostly on sheer talent alone, with very little practicing.

Chuck was definitely one of those difficult pieces to fit in the puzzle to make the picture complete. But Iowa State's coach Harold Nichols was able to do so. He had many pieces to work with to make one complete puzzle for many years. It wasn't perfect, but Nichols, like Coach Siddens, put those different puzzle pieces together and created winning teams out of them many times. Years later, I was able to do the same because I had so many great teachers.

A Special Place

In early to mid-June in 1971, I was staying in a cabin supervising and teaching young wrestlers in church camp facilities along West Okoboji Lake near Okoboji, Iowa. At this point, my main focus was on training to become a World and Olympic champion wrestler, but even though this wasn't a formal training camp at the USA level, it was great for me in several ways. I was living in spartan facilities, and all of my focus was on wrestling development and training.

Dave Martin, who had been one of my roommates at Iowa State, ran the camp, and he gave me a few teaching duties, but mostly just allowed me to train. The other wrestling counselors and teachers were all great workout partners, so I got some high levels of training in. Plus, most of the wrestling training was done in a church, so I felt like someone was looking out for me.

I was also learning new training tricks, even though I didn't fully understand them. During one of my first days there, wrestling training was about over for the day and I was a little hotter than usual. I let my instincts take over and walked out the door down to a dock on the lake a mere thirty yards away. After quickly undressing (except for my briefs), I jumped into the cold, clear lake water.

Wow! What a great feeling that was. I stayed in the water for a couple minutes and then got out. Then I jumped back into the lake again and took a quick exit back onto the dock and sat down in a chair. After sitting for a short period, I realized how quickly I had recovered and that I was ready to go back to training. So I grabbed a clean, dry shirt and went back to the wrestling mats. Even though I was almost finished with wrestling training for the day, I was able to go longer than normal, and I still felt good while doing so. Science was working for me, but that was over my head at the time. What I knew came from the on-the-job training that I learned through practice and experience.

Those dips became more regular during the next two weeks, depending on my need to recover.

At the end of the day after these wrestling workouts, I would change from wrestling shoes to running shoes and would have another counselor drive to pick me up after about ten or fifteen minutes of running. The thing is though, the people who were supposed to pick me up must have been playing *my own* mind games on me, for as the time got closer to when I thought they were going to appear, time seemed to stretch on longer. Still, I didn't let up on my pace. The more I thought they were sure to be there, the faster I ran.

If the object of their game was to encourage me to not let up, even at the end of a full day, it certainly worked. That ten-to-fifteen-minute run ended up being closer to thirty or forty minutes by the end of the two weeks of camp. Thanks, guys, for toughening me up!

A little sidenote about that summer in Okoboji: I've seen a photo of me on the dock after one of my recovery splashes. This was simply of me getting out of the water and sitting and recovering before going back to wrestling training in the church. In my view, there are some girls sunbathing on the dock right next to the camp's dock. Believe it or not, one of these girls was Kathy, my future wife, hanging out with her girlfriends. Of course, this group of girls had very little effect on my training. At that point in time, my mind was always, or at least mostly, on wrestling.

Okoboji continues to be a special place for many. For me, it was mostly the time spent at the camp that was special, but with continual connections of that dock shot (Kathy) and with people like Don and Jane Mittelstadt (Tom Brands's wife Jeni's parents) living there, along with former Iowa student wrestling volunteer, Julie Fillenwarth, and her family resort, the place still rocks. Of course, the lake helps!

3

Show Me the Way: The Peterson Brothers

The environment one grows up in and continues to put oneself in often determines a person's outcomes.

In the spring of 1968, Ben Peterson was finishing his senior year in high school in Cumberland, Wisconsin. He wasn't on the radar of many big wrestling schools after finishing in second place in his weight division at the Wisconsin high school state wrestling tournament. But the 1968 Olympic wrestling trials were in Ames, Iowa, on the campus of Iowa State University, and Ben qualified to come through a regional wrestling event. Of course, his name did not stand out among the many older, credentialed athletes in the group, but Iowa State head wrestling coach Harold Nichols watched the trials and something about Ben struck him. Coach Nichols offered him a partial scholarship after the trials, which Ben accepted. He knew of the wrestling program's reputation for excellence, but Iowa State was the best match for his academic interests.

Ben started wrestling at Iowa State during my second year of eligibility in wrestling. I was coming off an individual NCAA title, and was always looking for good workout partners. Ben turned out to be a great one for me, even though he was considerably bigger (I wrestled at 137 pounds, and he wrestled at 190 pounds). He had an attitude that kept me alert and intense during practice sessions. He could always come back for more, and we could battle every day if needed. He helped me a lot physically, but I probably helped him more. Working out together, he took on a new and higher level of commitment. Of course, I could probably say the same, because I now had a partner who would do many of the extras alongside me. I have found that having a good, motivated partner always helps with training. In high school, I had Doug Moses. In college, I had Ben Peterson helping me—and the entire Iowa State team—to victory.

Ben learned to adopt goals of higher magnitude being around a roomful of highly motivated recruited wrestlers. He did the same with his academics. Beyond that, not much changed with his already disciplined life as a devout Christian. At the end of his freshman year, Ben had a precise goal of capturing the starting position in his weight class the next season—and he did. He wrote the motivating words of his competition on a chalkboard in his house so that he woke to that daily.

Like Doug Moses, Ben went on to even higher levels of achievement on the mat. He was a three-time All-American, two-time national champion, and went on to win two Olympic medals: gold at the 1972 Munich Olympics and silver in the 1976 Montreal Olympics. He also qualified for the 1980 Olympic team, which boycotted the Moscow-based event due to the Soviet Union's invasion of Afghanistan. Ben earned a bronze medal at the 1973 World championships as well.

Who's even more unbelievable is Ben's older brother John, who didn't win any high school state wrestling tournaments and didn't win national championships in college at the University of Wisconsin–Stout. John came to train at Iowa State after college, and he saw how Ben and I were working. He began training with the two of us, and he started to improve quickly. It didn't take long for John to realize his potential in an atmosphere focused on hard work and dedication.

I had been planning to live by myself the year after I won the World championships, but I invited John to live with me instead. In that year of living with me and working out with all of us, John just kept getting better and better. He went on to win the 1972 Olympic silver and the 1976 Olympic gold, and he ending up medaling twice at the World championships: bronze in 1978 and silver in 1979.

"I've said over and over that if it hadn't been for that invitation to come down and train at Iowa State, there is no way I would have ever made the Olympics," John says now. "I was a good NAIA wrestler. I'm sure I had the ability to win the national tournament, but didn't. Dan helped my confidence come way up.

"When we would work out together, I quickly found out that I couldn't keep up with this guy. He'd get me so tired and I'd get discouraged that I might not be in the same league as him. But I was determined that I was going to stick with it.

"There were times in practice where I felt humiliated about my performance, but the thing I really appreciated about Dan was that he never humiliated me. There are some guys who enjoy punishing people. Dan had a way of making me feel ashamed if I quit too early without ever saying a word or acting in a way that was degrading me. He let me know that you can't stop and you have to keep going. Little things he would say were really encouraging."

One never knows what he or she is capable of until they're put in the right atmosphere. Everyone should think hard about what they need to succeed and bring out the best in themselves.

I was the real winner in all this though, because the Peterson boys' strict lifestyle was great for me. An example of this is when John first moved in with me and we went on our first trip to the grocery store together. I bought a six-pack of beer along with other food items. The food was soon devoured, but when we moved out the following year, that same six-pack was still in the fridge. I didn't eliminate beer completely that year, but since John didn't drink, I apparently never did so in the space I shared with him. Both brothers set a good example for me in terms of leading a good life and developing a stronger faith in my beliefs.

Iowa State to Iowa:
The Move in Hindsight

In early December 1971, my dad came to visit me in Ames. During his visit, he told me that Gary Kurdelmeier, then the assistant wrestling coach at Iowa, wanted to meet with me.

"What for?" I asked.

"Dave McCuskey, the current coach, is retiring, and Gary is moving up to be the new head coach. He wants you as the new head assistant," he said.

"He doesn't even know me," I pointed out.

"Pretty much everybody knows you in wrestling."

"How could that be?" I responded. "I can't remember talking to him."

In the end, I agreed to have lunch with Kurdelmeier in Ames. He was coming to me, so our meeting didn't have to disrupt my training time. The Olympics were just nine months away, and every day counted.

My dad came down for the meeting as well, and we all met over lunch in between workouts at a local family restaurant away from campus. It was kind of an unknown place, where little was going on. Gary basically offered me the job on the spot. He told me to take my time and that there was no pressure to make a decision anytime soon. That was fine by me, as I had a big Russian trip coming up in a few weeks, and my main thoughts were simply, "Beat the Russians."

I did beat the Russians, and with very little, if any, thoughts on my professional life beyond the Olympics in September. But while I wasn't thinking about this offer much, there was a lot going on behind the scenes, both in Ames and Iowa City.

Coach Nichols had hired Jon Marks from Iowa City to work in his private business selling wrestling products, like shoes and mats. Much later, we learned that Jon had Kurdelmeier connections that weren't known at the time, and that he was really there to serve as a "plant" or a spy for Iowa and Kurdelmeier.

Jon started coming to our practices, and he also became good friends with some of my closest buddies and me. He was a big guy, and when I couldn't find enough guys to train with, he volunteered to suit up with me to help me get a wrestling workout. He must have had some wrestling background, because he knew how to push and lean into me to give me good work on snapping my opponents and setting them up for scoring. Of course, he got tired fast, which meant he needed to go in short bursts, and if I needed him a second time, I had to let him rest and alternate with someone else.

My wrestling was going well, and I was staying on track with my goals. But then I injured my knee in the middle of February when I gave a workout partner too much of an advantage to start because I knew I could. I forgot that most injuries happen when you're in less control than you should be. It was stupid on my part, especially since I had a match with a good Soviet wrestler four days later.

I thought the injury would go away overnight, but it kept me up all night, and in the morning, it was worse. I could not move. I started crying since I knew I had to call and cancel my appearance at the meet. It was very difficult since I'd never backed out of a wrestling event before. I called Coach Myron Roderick, who was hesitant at first, but it didn't take him long to realize that I must be really injured. He knew me well and knew I wouldn't back out of something unless I really had to. It's the only match I ever missed in twelve years of wrestling competition.

Now, any thoughts on my future with the University of Iowa moved even further back in my mind. My focus was now on my injury and getting back on track to winning the Olympics.

My next meeting with the University of Iowa was at the Iowa state high school wrestling tournament in Des Moines. I met with Kurdelmeier again, along with Iowa supporter Roy Carver, CEO of Bandag from Muscatine, Iowa. Roy was pretty forward at this meeting and asked me what help I needed in making my decision, obviously suggesting that he would offer me money to accept Iowa's offer. This didn't help them though, because I told my family about it, and my mother, Katie, had a conversation with Roy shortly after and made sure he knew I wasn't for sale. My dad might have said something different, but my mom ruled in this area.

Two weeks after the state wrestling tournament though, something must have changed in Iowa City. I got a call asking me how my decision-making process was moving along. I really had not given it much more thought, especially with my injury, and I told them that. They seemed to understand, and told me to take my time.

But the very next day, I got another call, and apparently a change of plans had taken place on their end. Now, it was a take-it-or-leave-it offer, and it really upset me. So what did I do? In those days, my only path in making a decision was through my support systems—my family and friends. So that's where I went.

I called my parents and talked to my dad, explaining what was going on. He said, "Take it."

"Let me talk to Mom," I said.

She also told me to take it.

I was mad now. First of all, this decision wasn't supposed to be happening until much later. Second, why was everyone telling me to take the offer when I wanted to stay at ISU?

"I'm calling my friends," I told my parents.

But all of my friends said the same thing: "Take it."

I had been communicating with Coach Nichols through this whole process, and he had also set up meetings for me with the Iowa State athletic director. They didn't feel threatened, for they knew my strong loyalty to Iowa State. But with a take-it-or-leave-it choice facing me, and *all* of my support systems on board with Iowa, my decision was more or less made. Especially because, right then, all I wanted to focus on was Munich and nothing else.

I accepted Iowa's offer, but Coach Nichols and the ISU athletic department quickly came back to reverse my decision. My word to Iowa held though, even though I had not signed a contract yet. For me, the backing and stamp of approval of my family and friends were as good as a contract. The University of Iowa had clearly done their homework in terms of knowing whom I relied on. When they knew my support system was on board for Iowa, they knew it was time to strike. They certainly did, and I bit!

Not long after this, Jon Marks was nowhere to be found in Ames, for as soon as I accepted UI's offer, he packed up in Ames, left town, and moved back to Iowa City. He went to work at the University of Iowa for Bob Brown in therapeutic recreation, and worked part-time for the wrestling program, especially with its recruiting efforts. It wasn't until a couple of years later that I learned of Jon's role in my coming to Iowa City.

■ ■ ■

At the time of my move to Iowa City, wrestling had very few regulations compared to what has happened in the years since. I think the prominence of Iowa's program over the past forty years has helped bring the sport to a higher role and prominence within the NCAA. We started breaking lots of attendance records, and more people started becoming full-time administrative workers in the sport. This also came about at a time when other issues were causing athletic departments to drop sports. With wrestling getting more notice, it has survived many of its difficulties, but it still seems to always need to stay ahead of the rest.

Like my move from wrestler to coach, others in the sport have helped further the cause. Cael Sanderson's move from Iowa State to Penn State and the rise in prominence of their program, with four straight NCAA titles from 2011 to 2014 and two more titles in 2016 and 2017, have brought further valuable attention to the sport, especially in the East. Tom Ryan, coach of Ohio State, did some of the same with their 2015 NCAA championship. Coach J Robinson's move to Minnesota from Iowa sparked lots of interest, and they put their program on the map with NCAA titles. Of course, Oklahoma State's prominence and Coach John Smith's success and NCAA titles have the longest history. The University of Iowa with its mass of titles still currently stands out the most, especially with the record-breaking attendance in Iowa's outdoor football stadium, at 42,267-plus at a dual against Oklahoma State—Grapple on the Gridiron was a great success.

When wrestling coaches move, it has often turned out well for the sport, as it brings lots of attention, both locally and nationally. My own move in October 1972 from Iowa State to Iowa was certainly calculated by lots of people, but it was good for the sport.

5

Life Directions

At the end of March 1968, the Iowa State Cyclones finished in second place at the NCAA wrestling tournament. It was a tight loss, one that Iowa State could have won with a full team in place, but one of our top performers left the team not long before the competition. I took first in the 130-pound weight class, but my final match against the University of Oklahoma's returning NCAA champion David McGuire wasn't easy. He was a tough, determined guy.

Shortly after the NCAA tournament, the Olympic trials were held in Ames, Iowa. I wasn't sure whether to wrestle in this event, even though I had qualified. The morning of weigh-ins on the first day of competition, I decided to wrestle at 138.5 pounds, since the weight was easy to make. I ended up in third place behind Bobby Douglas and Tom Huff, but it was an event that gave me important feedback for my future.

It taught me that to win at this high level of competition, it isn't enough to just show up. I needed to prepare like I always had, physically and mentally. I had just showed up and wrestled with no real focus on the event, and I did not like the outcome. That experience positioned my vision differently for the future, and my commitment to wrestling at the highest level increased.

"Dan and I trained together, so I knew his training habits, and I knew he was a hard worker," remembers Bobby Douglas, member of the US Olympic teams in 1964 and 1968. "I was the assistant coach at Iowa State, so we worked out together. I knew he had the ability and the desire to do what was needed to be the best.

"I thought Dan would do exceptionally well at the international level if the officiating didn't get in his way. In order for that to happen, you had to dominate, and he was dominant to the point where officiating wasn't a factor. Americans were getting hosed all the time in international competition, and sometimes it wasn't the officials who were doing it; sometimes it was the wrestlers buying and selling matches.

"Dan was an easy guy to like. I respected his work ethic. His mind was focused on one thing and one thing only, and that was wrestling. He had the work ethic, and he also had the support. His family supported him."

I spent the summer of 1968 in Alamosa, Colorado, training with the Olympic team, and it brought my effectiveness to new levels. One can tell by my scores both before and after that summer. The level of mental commitment led to an increase in physical commitment both on and off the mat, which led to being more dominant on the mat.

Fast forward to November 1975, and I was in a similar dilemma. I was in my third year as an assistant coach for the Hawkeyes, and I decided to wrestle at the Northern Open in Madison, Wisconsin. I decided to wrestle up a weight (158 pounds instead of 150 pounds) because our team needed to improve at this weight class, so I filled in for this competition. Besides, I was getting some pressure from the United States Wrestling Federation to wrestle again.

To determine where my heart really was, I wrestled the event. After the first match, I knew. It just wasn't the same. After two and a half years of coaching, I could tell that my thrill was in coaching athletes to victory, not competing myself. I sat in the stands between matches with a neck brace on and decided I would just finish what

I had started and then be done with it. It didn't even cross my mind that I would lose a match. I was still confident in my abilities, but I didn't take into account that someone would actually try to beat me.

Here I was again, not ready for what life was throwing at me, and it made me vulnerable. As it turned out, Lee Kemp got a lot of bragging rights from that day when he beat me.

"I would not be who I am today without Dan Gable," says Kemp now. "I started wrestling in ninth grade, and I didn't know much about wrestling at the time. I went 11–8–3 after my sophomore season, and I really wanted to get better. My coach took me and a couple other wrestlers to a weeklong camp during the summer of 1972, the year Dan won the Olympics. I had a chance to be at this summer camp with all these great wrestlers, including Dan Gable. I knew very little about wrestling, but I knew I wanted to be like him. When Dan needed someone to demonstrate the moves, I jumped up, and I was the guy he demonstrated moves on for that whole week. I felt that just being around him, and having him demonstrate on me, I would learn the moves better.

"When the session was over, all the kids would go to lunch. I would miss lunch and sit there just to watch him train. I'd get up in the morning early just to watch him go for his run. I was trying to gain every little bit that I could from being around him.

"I went back home after that summer camp and replicated everything I saw. It was the running, the drilling, the wrestling—everything. I was undefeated that year and beat the defending state champion. That would not have happened without that weeklong camp with Dan Gable. He changed my life. He changed my thinking. That experience just flipped me upside down. He changed me forever, and I won state the next year too and went undefeated."

A year after he beat me at the Northern Open, Kemp and I met again. It was 1976, and I was an assistant coach for the US Olympic wrestling team, and Lee was an alternate for the team. One of the Olympic training camps was in Madison, Wisconsin, where Lee was a student. He tells the story better than I could, so I'll just let him tell it:

"At the end of the movie *Rocky III*, Rocky Balboa and Apollo Creed box in a ring without anyone around. In 1976 Dan and I had our own Rocky Balboa–Apollo Creed moment. I hadn't worked out with Dan since our match. We hadn't spoken to each other, but Dan wasn't a real conversationalist anyway.

"After one of the practices, my college wrestling coach told me that Dan wanted to wrestle, and I was excited about that. So I went in the room and he was just shadow wrestling. No words were said, and we did that Rocky thing. It was cool. In his mind he wanted to prove to himself that he could beat me still, and he did. He got the best of me.

"I grew in that practice, too, because I got to challenge myself to a level I'd never been challenged before. He was very intense. I learned how to never stop wrestling when you're on the edge. He never stopped wrestling when we were on the edge, against the walls, or against the benches. It wasn't anything negative; he just wanted to wrestle continuously. He didn't want to stop; he didn't want to give you a break. If you tried to take a break, he wouldn't give it to you. I learned in that practice how to be tough. He taught me that. After that practice it was like a weight was lifted off him for sure. For me, it was another challenge, because I had to get better, I knew I had to get better because I wasn't good enough to compete with him in the room."

Lee Kemp went on to win three NCAA titles at the University of Wisconsin (1976–78) and three World titles (1978, 1979, and 1982). He missed the 1980 Olympics because the US boycotted the Moscow-based games; otherwise, I'm certain an Olympic title would be included.

For my part, after our match at the 1975 Northern Open, my life would no longer be pulled in two directions, between wrestling and coaching. Focusing on just one area gives that direction more strength, as the results show. Besides, as head coach of the 1978 and 1979 World teams, Lee Kemp's gold medals are on my accomplishments list.

The Unexpected
Becomes Expected

I don't believe in luck; I believe in hard work and success. Success happens when lots of people are working hard together toward the same goal. Each person makes his or her own contribution to the whole, and when these contributions come together, it can seem like luck. This is because day-to-day excellence creates these opportunities that can feel like luck.

That said, there were a few times in my coaching career when I really felt like things came down to luck, or that someone was watching out for me from above. How else would these coincidences have happened and turned into such great success stories?

In the early 1970s, Gary Kurdelmeier put me in charge of the wrestling room training upon my arrival as head assistant coach. That was my baby, and I made sure to never miss a practice. A few months into that first year, our athletic director Bump Elliot called me into his office and said he wanted to do a favor for a friend and send me to a high school in Westfield, New Jersey, to be a speaker at their spring athletic banquet.

I told Bump that my main duty was wrestling practices and that I shouldn't miss one for this. He knew we were making good progress with the program, but his directive was that I *would* do this, even if it meant missing practice. So I missed a practice and was somewhat upset about it.

I went out to their banquet, which I actually enjoyed. As the evening progressed, I learned that the kid who had done the invocation was a wrestler named Chris Campbell. He had gone undefeated that year and won the state wrestling championship.

So I gave my speech, and awards were handed out to Chris and other athletes for various areas of achievement. Afterward, Chris came up to me and said, "I really liked your speech. I'd be interested in looking at the University of Iowa for my future for college."

I said, "So you were the undefeated state champion for this year?"

"Yeah."

"How did you do in your other years?" I asked.

"I just came out for my senior year," he said.

I was shocked. "So you just came out your senior year, went undefeated, and won a state championship?"

"Yes," Chris said, "I had dabbled in it earlier, but this was the first year I was on the team."

When I got back to Iowa City, I did some poking around and found out he had already committed to go to a smaller local school to wrestle, a good Division II school. I called their coach, whom I already knew. I didn't want to look like I was stepping in to take a recruit away from him, but I wanted to learn more about the kid. The coach told me, "Gable, if he wants to go to Iowa where you are, I'll gladly let him go there to compete at that level."

Chris still wasn't fully on my radar though. That summer, the USA National Junior Championships took place at the University of Iowa in the old Field House, and Chris Campbell entered it. He ended up getting second. After that, I figured this kid must be pretty good, so I offered him a small scholarship, and he became a Hawkeye.

"I had a great high school with a great athletic department," Campbell remembers. "It was well funded. They brought in Dan Gable as guest speaker right after the 1972 Olympic Games. When he was there, I went up to him and told him I could kick his butt.

He looked at me like I was a thug, but he smiled. I was a cocky little kid then.

"Nobody really knew about me. I wrestled as a sophomore on the junior varsity team. As a junior, I didn't go out for wrestling, so I only wrestled varsity my senior year. I won state that year, but no one really knew about me. They didn't realize what I could potentially be until junior nationals in the summer. I was going to attend a college in Maryland, but the coach told me that he wouldn't let me because I had too much talent. He said, 'There is this guy named Dan Gable, and you need to go out there and wrestle for them.' For some reason I believed him, and it was the best advice I ever got. I sold my car, which paid for my plane flight out. My first flight ever was to Iowa."

It wasn't too long before Chris moved up to more scholarship with us. He ended up being a three-time NCAA finalist, two-time NCAA champion, and a World champion in 1981. Then he got his law degree at Cornell, and nine years later, made a comeback in 1990, winning silver at the World championships, followed by a fifth-place finish in 1991. He won a bronze medal at the 1992 Olympics in Barcelona, just a few days shy of turning thirty-eight.

How's that for a trip I didn't want to take?

■ ■ ■

In the summer of 1983, a wrestling scholarship came in signed by an athlete. It wasn't much of a scholarship, but I hadn't approved it, so I tore it up and put it in the garbage. We had a great group of coaches and volunteer coaches at the time, but apparently my authority wasn't worth much to some members of my staff.

Anyway, that was a done deal as far as I was concerned, until I heard that the torn-up-scholarship recruit was coming anyway. I figured, well, if he wants to walk on, that's fine. I found out later that the coaching staff had typed up and sent out another small scholarship, and he signed. Now what was I going to do, fire my coaching staff? I gave in, but was not happy.

Things turned out very well in the end though. Brad Penrith of Windsor, New York, was a three-time NCAA tournament finalist, 1986 NCAA champion, 1991 World silver medalist, and is the former head wrestling coach at the University of Northern Iowa. He is now a divisional department manager for Mudd Advertising in Cedar Falls, Iowa, and has a great family.

Whether that was luck or not, thank coaches J Robinson and Jon Marks (RIP).

■ ■ ■

My final year as head coach was strange, with a lot of odd pieces that came together to make a spectacular whole. It was like a script God had put together.

Every year, the wrestling team put out a promotional poster with the season schedule, and the 1997 team had plenty of current material to splash on that year's poster. All of the returning All-Americans were pictured, and there was one picture that represented the as-yet unknowns who would step up. The photo was of an unidentified wrestler getting his arm raised. Only his back and head could be seen, and this unknown wrestler represented the next NCAA champion.

We had a lot of firepower returning that year, but it was a struggle, both with my health and the team's performance. The University of Northern Iowa hosted the NCAAs that year in Cedar Falls, located next door to my hometown of Waterloo. We weren't the favorite to win, but we gave it our all and dominated in record-breaking fashion. It was a real spectacle, everybody came through, and it happened right in the area where I grew up. It was an incredible ending for my coaching era.

The real shocker came years later though, when I was reviewing old poster schedules and noticed the final year's unknown-raised-hand photo. It turns out that that hand belonged to Hawkeye wrestler Jessie Whitmer. In 1997, Jessie was a fifth-year senior who had been wrestling behind Mike Mena at the lightest weight his whole collegiate career. Mena decided to move up a weight class after the season started, and so it was Jessie Whitmer who stepped up and won the NCAA title. For his part, Mena made it to the finals at the weight class above, but Jessie "the Strongest Man in the World" became the talk of the tourney.

As a wrestler, once Jessie had a few matches under his belt (or, in this case, under his singlet), I noticed that he was doing moves that weren't supposed to work, yet they did for him. His power and positioning overwhelmed and replaced the normal skills that were needed for execution. This seldom happens, and it contributed to his NCAA victory that year.

"When we were doing that poster, it was either going to be me or 177-pounder Tony Ersland, and Coach Gable picked me," says Whitmer today. "I don't know if he had any foresight in why he chose me, because at the beginning of the year, he told me I was going to win the national tournament at 118 pounds. He obviously had a lot more belief in me than I had in myself. Throughout the year, he instilled his belief in me. By the end, it felt like it was going to happen, and it did happen."

The unknown photo on that poster still blows my mind, but that seems to be normal for my life. The unexpected often turns out so well that it becomes expected.

Mama's Boys

Early in my career as an assistant coach at Iowa, during the 1972 to 1973 wrestling season, two former Iowa wrestlers, Rob Machacek and Doug Duss, bought a piece of land beneath another bar on Dubuque Street in downtown Iowa City. They wanted to open their own bar, but there was a problem: this piece of land under another business was only a crawl space. Obviously, they needed to get it dug out so the bar could be created. This was no easy task, but when you are part of a wrestling team, you have access to people who know how to work hard and do things others would probably never consider.

Rob asked guys from the wrestling program to help by getting into that crawl space and start digging. It wasn't going to be difficult mentally, but it was definitely a tough job physically. Personally, I wasn't sure if I should join in, because I had just won the Olympics, and I wasn't sure how close Coach Kurdelmeier wanted me to be with the team in my new role as assistant coach. I also felt that the community was keeping a close eye on me. Remember, we *were* helping build a bar.

Wearing gloves and dust masks, the Hawkeyes initially had to pull themselves under the floor of the business located above. Once inside, the guys started digging using picks, small shovels, and their hands as they fought their way through the dried clay and rocks. The dirt and rocks were pushed onto a manual conveyor belt that carried everything outside to the sidewalk, where another group of guys carried that load to the bed of a nearby truck. The driver of the truck and a few workers would then haul everything away to be dumped. The system, as difficult as it was, was successful because these wrestlers were used to hard, physical work and didn't shy away from it.

Dan Holm wrestled for Iowa from 1972 to 1975 and helped with the creation of the bar that would later be dubbed Mama's. For his part, Holm was a three-time All-American (1973–75) and an NCAA champion in 1975. "Climbing under the floor and working was a unique experience," Holm remembers. "We had lights down there, and it was noisy from the conveyor belt. It was one of those things where you just kept plugging away, like a one-step-at-a-time kind of project."

Once the wrestlers had dug down several feet, walls were poured with cement. This helped secure the ceiling of the business above us. In some ways, this was a backward project: normally, when you build a large room, you go from the floor, upward. Here, we were forced to go from the ceiling, downward.

As the project moved along, some wrestlers, including Holm, used it as a way to add to their training. "I needed to lose some weight to make 150 during this time, my sophomore year," Holm recalls. "I also knew they needed to get as much work done as possible. I decided to implement this into my day. I'd go to school and sometimes do some morning training. Then I'd have a day full of classes, followed by wrestling practice and sometimes weight lifting."

For most people, this would be a full day of work, but these were Iowa wrestlers. As Holm explains, "In the evening, I'd go out for a run, and usually that run led me to Mama's after a few miles. I would be wearing a cotton sweat suit, with a plastic sweat suit over that, followed by another cotton sweat suit. When I'd get to Mama's I'd just jump in and start digging.

"I wasn't the only wrestler who did this," he adds. "A lot of the guys did this. We had to get our weight down, and there was work to do. It was a great combination."

Eventually, after months of digging, the walls were in place ten feet down, and the floor and ceiling were in place. From there, all that was left was to add the interior of Mama's.

The "Mama's Boys" were definitely making progress on the mats, as well as with the pick and shovel. That 1973 season, we moved up in the standings, followed by winning the Big Tens in 1974. Then in 1975, we won our first NCAA team championship at Princeton. A *Sports Illustrated* writer had heard about the Mama's experience, and when the magazine came out, the headline about us winning the national championship read, "And the Winners Were Mama's Boys."

Mama's, after it opened, became a regular hangout for Iowa wrestlers and wrestling fans. John Bowlsby, a recruit who joined the Hawkeyes for the 1975 season, talked about the impact Mama's had on the area. According to Bowlsby, an All-American in 1975, 1977, and 1978, "When you'd go down the stairs to Mama's, you could see by the third or fourth step who was in Mama's, or if you were already there, who was coming down the stairs."

My wife, Kathy, still remembers Mama's with fondness: "We were first married, and we didn't have any children for those first three years, and after practice we'd go get something to eat. Often we would go to Mama's. They had really good pizza there.

"There was one time where we got a little crazy," Kathy remembers. "I don't remember what we were celebrating, but there were these pipes, I think they were water pipes that hung down from the ceiling, and I remember just swinging on these pipes. It's a great memory."

For many years, Mama's was a beacon for finding members of the wrestling team. "Back in those days when I'd come into town, I'd call my friends from the team," Bowlsby says. "Now remember, this is long before the cell-phone era. So if your friend wasn't at home, the next place you'd call was Mama's, because more often than not, that was where you'd find them. The wrestlers were either practicing or competing, at home, or at Mama's."

Today, Mama's is called the Dublin Underground, but the memory of the wrestlers lives on in the bar. Even after all these years, Mama's remains a great part of the Iowa Hawkeye wrestling legend.

8

Royce, Mark, and Bruce: The Toughest, the Smartest, and the Hardest Worker

I've seen a lot of tough wrestlers and hard workers come through Iowa's wrestling room, but I think I would call Royce Alger the toughest wrestler I ever coached. Several things go into this, and I can't put my finger on just any one thing that makes him stand out in my mind as the toughest.

Maybe it was the story about how a tractor tipped over on him as a kid, trapping him in a ditch of water with his body pinned (excuse me: trapped, not pinned!) and his head just above the water for some time.

"I was ten years old, and my brothers and I were going to jump-start one of the tractors," Alger recalls. "It wasn't a very smart move. My brothers were going backward, so I pushed as hard as I could, but I was sliding and going so fast, I ended up jumping off it. I jumped as far as I could, but the tire spun me under. I had two hundred stitches, and it about took my leg off. They wanted to amputate it, but my mom wouldn't let them. She told them with my spirit, I wouldn't be happy with one leg."

From the looks of the scar on his leg, you would think wrestling, especially dominant wrestling, would be out of the question, but I never saw any evidence of this accident holding Royce back.

Maybe it was the time Royce had knee surgery, and within a week he wrestled in a big Iowa versus Iowa State dual in Ames.

"I blew my knee out during the last takedown of the last match on our eastern swing," Alger remembers. "I was a junior in college, and I just beat Greg Elinsky of Penn State, a two-time NCAA tournament runner-up, and on the way home, we wrestled against Ohio State. I was fifteen-pointing the guy, and my knee locked and it wouldn't come out.

"During the next day or two, it unlocked. I was getting ready for Kevin Jackson [of Iowa State] and Gable brought [former 190-pound NCAA champion] Pete Bush into practice that day. Pete did goofy stuff and was a big, tough guy. We went at it, and my leg locked again, and it did not unlock.

"They carried me out of the wrestling room, down the steps, and I went right in that day for surgery, and it was still locked. I was still in my workout gear. I actually showered in the hospital. We were going for our tenth straight title that year, and we needed me for that next dual. I had the surgery, and I wrestled eight days later. The doctors didn't want me to wrestle, but I had a good relationship with the trainers. I told them to just throw a bunch of that bubble wrap on it. I remember it hurting a little bit, but it wasn't hurting too bad to worry about that."

In spite of just having had surgery, Royce delivered a thrilling come-from-behind win against an outstanding opponent and gave Iowa much-needed team points.

Royce was also the reigning NCAA champion at 167 pounds and the team needed extra help to win the next year's team championship. I asked him to wrestle at 177 pounds. He did, and he won the title, but we just missed first place, getting second. He definitely wrestled his part though!

On the not-so-good side, one time at an early morning run in

Carver, I had to send Royce home for reporting to practice directly from a night out on the town. He needed his sleep more than he needed to abuse his body. Royce was one of the few wrestlers who could miss a practice and actually make up for it. I never believed in that for myself, or for others, until I coached Royce. He had what he called "rocket fuel," and could actually put everything he had into one thing so he didn't have to do it twice.

"Rocket fuel just means I have a different gear," Alger explains. "I'm a power guy. A lot of times when we'd go up for sprint laps, I'd always win the first sprint lap. I'd win it on the fourth one and maybe the seventh. I'd always tell them that I was working with rocket fuel. I was power. I was built a little bit different."

This power actually worked against him one night in Mount Vernon, Iowa, three miles from his home of Lisbon, Iowa. Coming out of a local bar after having overdone it a little, he was abruptly stopped on the street by local police and was asked for his identification. Being extremely popular in the area, Royce asked the officer, "You don't know me?" The officer said that he didn't, so Royce figured he could get away unidentified on foot. He turned, the rocket fuel kicked in, and *bam!* He ran straight into a big oak tree at full speed, knocking himself unconscious. Needless to say, after that they were able to identify him.

Royce was labeled a powerful wrestler who competed extremely hard. But when you analyze his wrestling skills, he had great technique that most people never gave him credit for. Snaps, go-behinds, leg sweeps, inside trips, knee taps, bear hugs, cut doubles, elbow pass to leg tackles, and near-wrist rides to pins were just a few skills included in his bag of tricks. Not bad for "just a tough guy."

Today, Royce has a good job that allows him the freedom to also work with our high-end wrestlers. He seems to work well with all kinds of people involved in wrestling: athletes, coaches, administrators, and donors.

■ ■ ■

I would call Mark Mysnyk the smartest of my wrestlers. He was on our first 1975 NCAA championship team as the starting lightweight (118 pounds). Mark came to us from Vestal, New York, with two New York state wrestling titles and two US national freestyle championships, and he set the tone for the team both on the mat and in the classroom. He majored in general science, and graduated with a 3.99 GPA after his string of solid As was broken by a single credit hour of softball where he got a B.

Mark fit in very well at Iowa with our emphasis on discipline and hard work. He competed extremely hard, and his positive influence affected everyone on the team. Depending on whom I'm thinking about, this could mean keeping his teammates from getting into serious issues in the community, getting a higher grade on a test or in a whole class, walking away from a fight instead of getting into one, staying after practice and working a little extra, or being on-weight instead of over. A good, solid influence like Mark's spreads and makes the entire environment more disciplined, which leads to better performance for everyone.

"Wrestling for Dan did a couple things," says Mysnyk. "When I came to Iowa, I was a hard worker and disciplined, but being exposed to Gable elevated that to another level. I was disciplined, but I had a standard of discipline before me that was even greater.

"I don't know if I was the smartest. I think I maximized my opportunities scholastically better than average. I don't think I maximized my wrestling abilities. I think I could have done better on the mat, but I think I maximized the scholastic opportunities, and that's what the Iowa program is all about."

Of course Mark could have done better in his wrestling; our motto is "You can always get better." For that matter, look at his GPA. It could have been a 4.0 instead of a 3.99. But that doesn't change the fact that he was both an outstanding wrestler and student and a disciplined hard worker who positively affected everyone else on the team.

After wrestling, Mark went to medical school at the University of Iowa. He is still practicing orthopedics in Iowa City. It's only appropriate that his family life outdid even his wrestling and professional success. There are no Bs there!

■ ■ ■

I would call Bruce Kinseth my hardest worker. He came from a family who did well in their profession, the hotel business, and raised their children well. I heard about Bruce through one of my best friends, wrestling coach Larry Munger. Larry said to me, "You need to watch this kid. There's something about him. He's really tough on top." Bruce wasn't a big name in the recruiting world, so I was somewhat hesitant. But in reality he was exactly what we were looking for to add to the pool of good recruits.

I had a hard time getting hold of him though, because every time I called, he was working out. So I decided to skip the call and visit him directly in Decorah, Iowa. Even with my scheduled visit, he was out running when I arrived. After my visit, I was completely sold on him and his lifestyle.

He made an immediate impact his freshman year with his work ethic and overall positive attitude, but he still had work to do, especially in the down position. A good wrestler has to be able to escape in scholastic and collegiate wrestling or he is going to have a tough time. Bruce had some trouble with the escape, but he knew that and kept working at it. Bruce quickly became the leader in the room in terms of working the hardest, especially near the end of practice, when he just kept going, doing all the extras. He really raised the bar in this area for the whole team at practice.

After his freshman year, I still wasn't sure about Bruce and where he was heading in his wrestling career. Bruce went home to Decorah for part of the summer, and my family has a cabin about forty minutes away from Decorah, so I occasionally called him from the cabin to check on him. I also needed a wrestling workout, and he told me he had a wrestling room where he lived. His family lived in the hotel they owned in town, the Cliff House, and Bruce got them to turn one of the rooms into a wrestling room. He invited me up so we could both get a good workout in.

Bruce's wrestling room at the hotel was wall-to-wall mats. I had wrestled him a number of times during his first year, so I knew what to expect. But it had been a month or so since I had worked out with him, and wow, it was a good workout! Maybe it was the home mat advantage?

On my way back to the cabin, I got an extra Mountain Dew for the ride. Bruce hadn't won that practice, but I knew then what he was capable of in the future. I remember talking to myself on that drive back, saying, "He's going to be good!" It wasn't going to be automatic, as he still needed to master the escape. It took him another year of work for that, but it did happen. He eventually mastered the sit-out with great hip and hand control to near perfection.

He placed second at the NCAA tournament as a junior in 1978. His senior year, he took first at the Big Ten tournament, and at the NCAA tournament, where he got the most pins and was named Outstanding Wrestler. He also pinned everyone at the Big Tens and the NCAAs, one of only three to ever do so.

"One thing that made the difference for me more so than anybody else was that I was Gable's size," says Kinseth. "My evolution through college is because there was a lot of wrestling with Gable after practice was over, because he was coaching all through practice, so he's not just wrestling. Let's say practice started at 3 P.M. and it was two hours; then it would be time for Gable to keep someone after practice. I was never done when practice was over. When I lived in the dorms, I barely made it back before the cafeteria closed at seven at night. I wrestled with the team all practice, and I wrestled with Gable after, and then would go down to the sauna and unwind, and then sprint over to the dorms to eat before the cafeteria closed. You'd get into some really long workouts, which were the best thing for me to get better.

"I actually liked to wrestle. I loved to practice. That's what made it easy to be a hard worker. I liked to be the king of the room and beat up anybody I could. I gradually developed that over all the years I was there. If someone wanted to slack off, they wouldn't call on me. If they wanted to get better and work hard, then they'd come to me. Wrestling a lot was the key thing for me.

"It was as much about the journey. I loved being around wrestling. I loved being around the wrestlers. I loved being around hard workers. I loved being around Dan Gable. I was fortunate to be around that environment where I was a product of it. If I'd have gone to another college, I probably wouldn't have been that successful, because I wasn't that great of an athlete. I was a piece of soft putty that they molded. Practicing all the time made the difference for me."

But for me, my athletes' real success is in where they are now and what they are accomplishing today. Bruce has a strong family life, and his family's hotel business has expanded from the Cliff House in Decorah to many hotels across the country. Clearly, he is still working hard, and he was never soft putty when he wrestled for me.

With my wife, Kathy, after our first year of marriage. We're still going strong at forty-three years together, thanks to a lot of hard work, communication, patience, and love of family. Photo courtesy of the Gable family.

Our family didn't start with just me and Kathy. And it goes beyond the Carpenters, Gables, and Leamings. It also depends on the Mitchells, Gavins, Olsztas, and the McCords. It will go on from here. Photo courtesy of the Gable family.

This picture sums up two things I hold close to my heart: the outdoor lakes of Minnesota, and most important, what my mom thought of me. Photo courtesy of the Gable family.

Hometown celebration at McElroy Auditorium with my mom and dad after the 1972 Munich Olympics. Photo courtesy of the Gable family.

Grandpa Charles Leaming, a man whom I wish I would have gotten to know better. Photo courtesy of the Gable family.

Cresco, my favorite small town in Iowa, is the home of the Iowa Wrestling Hall of Fame. There's only one thing missing from this mural (top): my early wrestling idol, Tom Peckham (bottom). Mural photo courtesy of the Iowa Wrestling Hall of Fame; Peckham photo courtesy of Iowa State University Library Special Collections.

Smart at coaching, smart at business, Harold Nichols was a coach who passed along solid advice about wrestling and life to his wrestlers and those who knew him. Photo courtesy of Iowa State University Library Special Collections.

I credit Chuck Jean with helping me shape the foundation of my coaching career by making me realize that every wrestler operates on an individual wavelength. Photo courtesy of Iowa State University Library Special Collections.

Coach Bobby Douglas, lifelong contributor to the sport—he even managed to enjoy it sometimes. Photo courtesy of Iowa State University Library Special Collections.

A great example of putting in the time both on the mat and in the classroom, Mark Mysnyk was the guy who did everything well. He was the one everybody looked up to. Photo courtesy of Department of Special Collections and University Archives, the University of Iowa Libraries.

Always reaching for new heights, Royce Alger is still contributing to Iowa and USA Wrestling. Photo courtesy of Department of Special Collections and University Archives, the University of Iowa Libraries.

One of my favorite all-time success stories, Bruce Kinseth, a decorated wrestler who is still setting records in life. Photo courtesy of Department of Special Collections and University Archives, the University of Iowa Libraries.

John Peterson (left) and Ben Peterson (right), two brothers who credit me for their strong wrestling performance, but I have to give them greater credit for keeping me focused on good life experiences. Photo courtesy of the Gable family.

Lee Kemp and I equally built on each other's experiences. I helped expose him to a new level of training, and he helped guide me to my calling as a coach. Photo courtesy of the Gable family.

J Robinson, Chris Campbell, and me: early years and good times. Lots of celebrations. Photo courtesy of the Gable family.

Grilling with Coach George Raveling at an Iowa wrestling promotional event. This night marked the last time I allowed a vice to steer my actions. Photo courtesy of the Gable family.

Anyone who knows me knows my love of saunas. Here I am enjoying a gift from my parents, surrounded by a few of my winning moments. Photo courtesy of the Gable family.

Mike DeAnna, putting on a typical great show for the Iowa fans in the old Field House. Photo courtesy of Department of Special Collections and University Archives, the University of Iowa Libraries.

Rico Chiapparelli, the Baltimore Butcher, never disappointed the fans when it came to putting on a good wrestling show. Photo courtesy of Department of Special Collections and University Archives, the University of Iowa Libraries.

Ray Brinzer was a unique character that the fans adored for good reason: his personality and wrestling brought them in. Photo courtesy of Department of Special Collections and University Archives, the University of Iowa Libraries.

Randy Lewis was a wrestler who inspired me to find my own inner confidence during moments of doubt through his unwavering support of my coaching. Photo courtesy of Department of Special Collections and University Archives, the University of Iowa Libraries.

With Brad Smith, I needed more experience to be able to handle his situation. Once I had that experience, he won the national championship in 1976. Photo courtesy of Department of Special Collections and University Archives, the University of Iowa Libraries.

Brooks Simpson, another beneficiary of my unique training methods. Photo courtesy of Department of Special Collections and University Archives, the University of Iowa Libraries.

Kevin Hogan saved the streak by being ready to perform in the 1993 Big Ten championships. Photo courtesy of *Amateur Wrestling News*.

Lincoln McIlravy, an all-time fan favorite who will never be forgotten. Photo courtesy of Department of Special Collections and University Archives, the University of Iowa Libraries.

Two coaches, two different views. Both needed for victory. Coach Gary Kurdelmeier deep in thought, and me reacting. Photo courtesy of University of Iowa Athletics.

Just a handful of the infamous wrestling season posters, the promotional brainchild of Coach Kurdelmeier. 1983, twelve individual national championship titles represented here, plus numerous World and Olympic medals. Posters courtesy of University of Iowa Athletics.

1985, J. R. Gable getting a little cocky and flaunting it maybe a bit too much. Poster courtesy of University of Iowa Athletics.

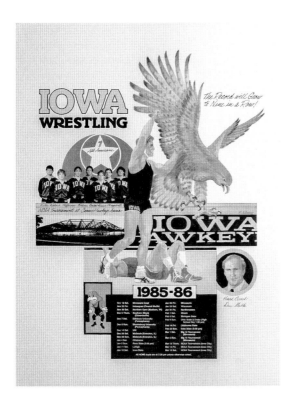

1986, a dominating ride that blindsided both me and the team to the hard fall that was about to come. Poster courtesy of University of Iowa Athletics.

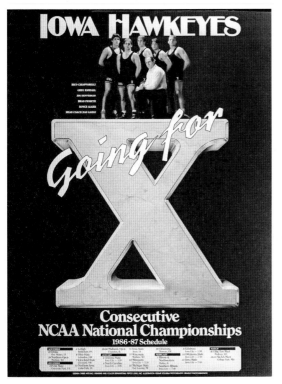

1987, definitely showing overconfidence to the point of needing to lose. Poster courtesy of University of Iowa Athletics.

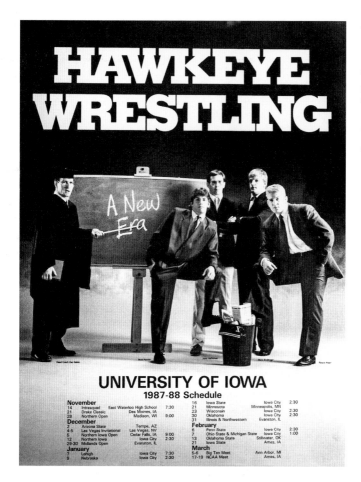

1988, when I finally had the courage to make some positive changes for the strength of the wrestling program. Poster courtesy of University of Iowa Athletics.

1992, fully loaded at ten weight classes with eleven All-Americans. Poster courtesy of University of Iowa Athletics.

Ten Miles × Two

If you lived in or near Iowa City in the fall of 1975, you might have seen something a little unusual in the evenings. Once a week, a set of headlights would head into town followed by the silhouette of a young man in a sweat suit running a few yards behind. It was Hawkeye wrestler Brad Smith's weekly ten-mile jaunt.

It was Brad's senior year, and up to that point in his career, he'd had some big wins and had ranked high, but he had never finished as an All-American.

With Brad's freshman class, we had given the incoming freshmen a questionnaire, and one of the questions on it asked if they were self-motivated or needed more motivation from the coaches. When he first entered our program, Brad Smith wrote, "I'm a self-motivated guy. Coach is there, but my self-motivation weighs more than the coach."

As Brad was going into his senior year, I looked back at his questionnaire and realized that I wasn't seeing any correlation between that answer and the person I'd seen training and wrestling. Something was wrong.

I pulled Brad aside one day and said, "We've been letting you do a lot on your own based on what you told us when you first came in here. It's not working. We need to make some changes."

Brad looked at me and responded, "When I filled out that form freshman year, I was intimidated and thought I needed to write what you wanted to hear. How could I tell you I needed help after I'd been a two-time state champion? I had to be this tough guy."

That made me think, *Wow! How many guys did we lose like this?* I needed to reevaluate this form.

For now, Kurdelmeier and I came up with a plan to help push Brad. He hadn't been finishing matches, so we decided that once a week, before it became too cold in Iowa, after practice I would drive him ten miles out of town and have him run back just to help build his stamina and endurance. We did that for about six weeks in a row. It was getting cold and dark by then, and Brad had already gone through a full practice, but he didn't complain. He just did it.

"At that point I was going into my senior year, and I felt like I could have been a two- or three-time All-American if I had wrestled to my capabilities," Smith remembers. "I thought I was in pretty good shape, but I had never been pushed past my comfort zone, and Dan was always good about doing those types of things: getting the most out of each wrestler and what they needed individually. Those ten-mile runs were what Coach Gable and Coach Kurdelmeier felt that I needed."

After those six weeks of ten-mile runs, Kurdelmeier gave Brad a big trophy that read, "First Place: Ten Mile Run."

Still, Brad didn't win a major tournament outright that year until the 1976 NCAA tournament in Arizona. There, he won the 142-pound weight class finals by eight points, a major decision. It all came down to helping him peak at the right time and finish his matches strong. Those ten-mile runs turned Brad Smith into the kind of wrestler he needed to be to win the NCAAs. It wasn't automatic. It wasn't even really a physical thing, as he was already a horse. Much of it was mental.

Today, Brad still remembers the importance of those runs and his extra training with me: "When he first came to Iowa, Gable didn't say much. He didn't talk a lot. He talked when he needed to. Before he became a head coach, he was a man of few words, but when he said something, you listened. Whatever he said left an impact on me for my career. I owe him a lot of credit for giving me a boost going into my senior year."

It was a great lesson in making the right kinds of changes to help each individual reach their potential. I don't know why it took me three years before I made a move like this to help an athlete reach his potential or overcome a flaw. It was a transition time for me: going from being an athlete to becoming a good coach. Catching this earlier would have helped Brad sooner, and we might not have needed those ten-mile runs. But maybe, just maybe, they gave Brad the insight he now has as a wrestling coach himself.

Brad went on to coach wrestling in Lisbon, Iowa, and at Iowa City High in Iowa City to a combined eleven Iowa high school state team titles. He is tied with Bob Siddens of West Waterloo for the most team titles in the state. He is still coaching today, and is back in Lisbon, Iowa, continuing to help young athletes reach their potential.

Brad Smith's success story involved him taking on a tough feat in order to conquer defeat, and it paid off for him. I love those kinds of endings and the principles learned from them. But it doesn't always turn out that way.

■ ■ ■

About a week before the beginning of the competition season in early November 1987, I decided to do weight checks on the team. Everyone was good except Brooks Simpson, our 190-pounder. He was about eight pounds over what I wanted him to weigh. With very little time before competitions started, I cracked the whip and told him I would help him get to where he needed to be quickly.

Every day for five days, I picked Brooks up at 6:30 A.M. and had him run ten miles before going about his normal day of classes and workouts. He basically ran from Iowa City to North Liberty on back roads all week while I drove beside him in a car, encouraging him.

At the end of the week, his weight was down to where it needed to be, but his ability to perform well on the mat was down as well. It was just too much, too fast. Brooks needed muscle and energy, and he didn't have enough time to get them back before he started competing. Running ten miles per day, five days straight, along with calorie restriction and normal workouts is not a good way to lose weight, especially if you plan on keeping your energy and power. Brooks's energy did come back, but his power didn't return until after the season was over.

This was a valuable lesson for the both of us, especially me because I'm the teacher, coach, and leader, and it cost both of us in performance. I tried to rectify it, but the damage had been done, and it stayed for most of the season.

"I didn't know enough to know it backfired," Simpson says now. "My endurance increased from those runs, but I do remember that this was above and beyond what the other guys were doing. I would come into practice later in the day, and I would get murdered. My strength wasn't up.

"I didn't realize that Coach Gable realized that it was a bad idea until about 2013. He said he made two mistakes with an athlete, and that I was one of them. He told me I had lost too much weight too fast, and I wasn't strong enough. I had no idea. I had absolutely no idea that he had come to that conclusion."

Brooks ended that year on a sour note at the Big Tens in Ann Arbor, Michigan. He was really upset when he lost the final match that kept him from advancing to the NCAA tournament. In the locker room immediately afterward, I made him look in the mirror to see the pain he was going through. I told him, "Look at that pain, remember that pain, and don't forget it for the future."

Brooks didn't forget it. It took a while, but he ended up being an NCAA finalist in the 1990 season, and I would say he is still going strong. Plus, that day in November 1987 was the last time he reported to the scales overweight. So maybe there was some good accomplished after all.

10

Equalizers Rule

Back in the early 1960s, wrestling coach Myron Roderick and his Oklahoma State wrestling team were winning most of the time. Roderick was the head wrestling coach at Oklahoma State from 1956 to 1969, winning seven NCAA team championships in thirteen years. In fact, Oklahoma State was the team to beat, and it was definitely a motivating name that helped drive me. Whenever I saw an Oklahoma license plate, I got a nervous high, whether I was in Iowa, Oklahoma, or anywhere.

Roderick understood the wrestling scoring system very well in terms of what areas of the sport a wrestler should master in order to win. His team played the "take-'em-down, let-'em-up, take-'em-down again" game. The rest of the country wanted to win, too, but instead of jumping on board with this philosophy, the NCAA made new rules to neutralize this system.

During the 1962–63 season, the NCAA rules committee implemented a new rule: the first takedown for each wrestler was worth two points, and any additional takedowns by that person had a value of one point. Because of this, a takedown now had the same value as an escape. The intention was to slow Oklahoma State down and to encourage more riding and more pinning. As a result though, the sport slowed down drastically, which was not helping wrestling's future. The rule lasted for only a year, and all takedowns returned to two points during the 1963–64 season.

This rule played out in a strange way during the 1963 NCAA wrestling tournament. Two wrestlers from Waterloo, Iowa, met in the finals of the 137-pound weight class. Bill Dotson from Iowa State Teachers College (now the University of Northern Iowa) faced Tom Huff of the University of Iowa. Dotson had graduated from East Waterloo High School in 1958, and Huff had graduated from West Waterloo High School in 1959.

Huff controlled the match early, but Dotson's conditioning played a factor after the match was tied 5–5 in regulation. Dotson eventually won 3–2 in overtime, becoming the first Division I NCAA wrestling champion in the history of East Waterloo High School.

"They were trying to stop Oklahoma State that year, and it happened to catch me, because I got two takedowns and he got one," remembers Huff.

J Robinson, a graduate assistant coach at the University of Iowa under Gary Kurdelmeier from 1973–76, and the top assistant under me from 1977–84, wrestled at Oklahoma State under Roderick. He saw Roderick's coaching philosophy play out in daily practices.

"Myron had a philosophy, and it stuck with me to this day, and that is that you have to have a philosophy about wrestling," Robinson says today. "People know a lot about wrestling, but they don't know how to put the pieces together to win championships.

"His philosophy was to take them down and let them go. If you can take someone down and get away from him, then you can beat anybody in the country. So that's all they did. All the years I was there, we never worked on riding, we never worked on pinning, we never worked on any of that stuff. All we worked on was different takedowns. That was it. The object was to take them down and let them go.

"If you break wrestling into five parts, then you spend twenty minutes on each part every day: reversals, escapes, takedowns, riding, and pinning. At Oklahoma State, you worked on takedowns sixty percent of the time and escapes forty percent of the time, so you're twice as good at getting away and three times better on your feet.

"The rules committee decided to beat Oklahoma State, so they changed the rules to get two for the first takedown and one for every subsequent takedown. The idea was to politically push Oklahoma State out, but then they changed it back the next season."

Punishing Oklahoma State for wrestling smart as well as hard, instead of just letting every team decide for themselves what was the best way to wrestle, put the sport on hold for a year. Every coach and wrestler need to coach and wrestle in the best and most entertaining way they can, and by legislating in this way, it slowed the sport down but helped prevent further growth of this kind of philosophy, for a while anyway.

In another example of this kind of thinking, in the mid-1970s, Coach Kurdelmeier and I wanted to keep wrestlers from going out of bounds. This would speed up the pace of a wrestling match and eliminate some of the stalling that was taking place. Iowa built a huge mat for a meet against Oklahoma. Wrestlers could not find the edge to get out of bounds because of the mat's enormous size. Within two weeks, the NCAA put a rule in place that set a maximum size on a mat.

"Gary took all of our mats out of the wrestling room, along with our meet mat, taped them together, and drew a big circle in the middle of it for the meet," says Robinson, who later led Minnesota to three NCAA team championships during his tenure there as head wrestling coach. "I think the circle was sixty-seven feet across. It was very evident when someone was trying to get to the edge of the mat because it was a long way from the center. The NCAA wrestling committee came back and decided that edge circles can be no more than forty-two feet.

"Kurdelmeier did all kinds of crazy stuff. He had an organ play at a dual meet one time, and it drove people nuts, but it got people talking about wrestling. That's what he did. He made wrestling an event."

Stan Abel, head wrestling coach at Oklahoma from 1973 to 1993, still remembers the meet with the oversized mat, and it was not a pleasant experience for him. He said it was like someone took his team out to an Iowa cornfield to wrestle.

"I remember how big the mat was and how the whole thing affected our kids that night, because we didn't wrestle very well," says Abel. "I made a comment after the match that Gable made a mat big enough that there was no place to run. I will say it was the biggest mat I've ever seen. It was very intimidating; I will tell you that."

For the most part, this big mat was a Gary Kurdelmeier promotional move, but having a big mat was fun while it lasted, especially since there were no edge-of-the-mat calls. It made the wrestling continuous, and it made for more action! I still think it showed more action in less time, but I actually know that it's not practical or possible to have these huge mats. Only two or three would fit into most arenas, when we often need eight standard-sized mats for our NCAA championships.

■ ■ ■

After I became head coach during the 1976–77 season, we occasionally got together as a team after matches and had a short workout to review our performance. We wanted to eliminate any flaws that we had during a meet. This did not last long though, as the NCAA immediately put a rule in place to stop practices after competition. However, while the coach could not have a formal practice after a meet, the individual athlete could do as he pleased. So, many continued the post-competition practices because they saw how valuable they were. This was the sign of a great team. Individuals doing what they need to do develop good habits and leadership skills. So in the end, this rule actually worked out better for us, but only because we were developing the athletes' minds for success, with or without the coaches. The athletes knew there would most likely be consequences for the team if they didn't follow through on these important and valuable procedures.

That's how championships are won. Members of the team must each know what they need to do for individual championship performances. In continuing these post-meet workouts on their own, our wrestlers were developing independence, a skill needed for life both on and off the mat.

■ ■ ■

Another equalizer happened when the season was over. More rules were added to keep coaches out of practices during this time period since they knew Iowa would be coaching athletes in freestyle wrestling, the style used in international competition. This didn't work out well for the sport as a whole, so we worked out a compromise within the rules to benefit everybody. Remember, in those days, wrestling and other Olympic sports were not as heavily regulated as sports like football and basketball.

It's difficult to legislate hard work because people competing at this level are used to governing their own lives twenty-four hours a day. You can accomplish a lot in twenty-four hours. Every time something is slowed down by the rules, there is a mind working to figure out how it can be done better under the current circumstances. Some people think legislation is always the answer to keep things equal and fair. It might be the easiest answer, but it definitely is not always the best answer. I believe that if matters were left in the hands of the experts, in this case, the people with years of actual proven experience, there is a much better chance for positive results.

Even rules concerning recruiting athletes are often altered based on the side of rejection. When I was recruiting Ed and Lou Banach in the late 1970s, I had orders from my administration not to check out of the hotel in their hometown until they made a decision on where they were going to college. With that in mind, I wasn't sure when I'd be back: it could be one day, two days, a week, a month— I would stay as long as needed to get a decision. It was a good ploy. Staying in their hometown and not leaving showed how much Iowa cared. Later, the administration told me that the thinking was that it would be hard to tell Dan Gable no in person.

"It was crazy," says Ed Banach all these years later. "There were a couple days when Dan was recruiting us hard. When Gable recruits you, it's like you are being courted. You want to go because he's going to help you accomplish your dreams.

"Dan was camped out for several days in Port Jervis, our hometown. He wanted wrestlers who wanted to be national champions and Olympic champions, and that's what we wanted.

"Dan didn't tell us that he wouldn't leave until he signed us, but it came out afterward in the papers. Our local paper interviewed Dan, and it got back to us that he wasn't going to leave until we signed with him."

It was a close decision for the Banachs. They had been split on their decision whether to attend Iowa or Lehigh. However, they made their decision fairly quickly with me in town, so it was definitely worth the extra few hours I spent in Port Jervis. The Banachs combined won five individual NCAA championships and two Olympic gold medals.

Of course, word got out about our tactic of me not leaving town until I had a commitment decision, and the NCAA enacted some new rules to curb that type of visit in the future. Still, even with these new rules in place, I was able to effectively recruit wrestlers in person.

For example, Kevin Dresser wrestled for the Hawkeyes from 1982 to 1986. My wife came along for the trip during my recruitment home visit with Kevin and his family in Humboldt, Iowa. The Dressers requested that we stay overnight in their home. We obliged their request, and Kevin signed on to wrestle at Iowa. Kevin placed fourth at the NCAA wrestling tournament in 1985 and was an NCAA champion in 1986. He is currently the head wrestling coach at Iowa State.

Bill Zadick of Great Falls, Montana, was another recruit who took an overnight stay to sign. "My best friend thought it was the biggest deal in the world," remembers Zadick. "He came over to the house and got Dan's autograph. He kept calling him 'Mr. Gable.' Dan came over to my house, and I signed my letter of intent. It was a big deal to have Dan Gable in Great Falls, Montana."

Besides an NCAA title, Bill went on to win a World championship in 2006 and is currently our national freestyle coach at USA Wrestling.

Rules are important, and usually they are put in place for good reasons. But this isn't always the case, as some are put in place because of a misunderstanding, or even because of political correctness. Legislating for equality is sometimes needed, but there is no legislation that can stop great work.

It's More Than Just a Name

Names can be impressive, and the motivation that one gets from them can be effective. But real results are based on actions, and productive actions are the ones that make a difference. So no matter who you are and what your name is, you are still you, and it is your actions that will define your life.

I remember standing in a funeral home in Waterloo, Iowa, talking with my dad, Mack, at my sister's funeral more than fifty years ago. Looking across the room, I saw an older gentleman viewing Diane's body. I had never seen the man before and asked my dad, "Who is that guy by the casket? He looks like you; is he a relative?"

My dad hesitated, then looked at me and said, "Dan, that is my real dad."

"What?" Obviously, I was shocked.

"Yes, that's your real granddad. Reverend Charles Leaming."

"Where has he been for the last fifteen years?" I asked.

"That's a story for another time. Right now, we have more important matters to deal with," he reminded me.

"You're right, Dad."

We hugged, and I put the matter aside. Being pretty naïve, and knowing that this was difficult enough for my family and friends, I went on with the business of Diane's funeral.

Looking back, you'd think I would have been curious or even mad about this discovery, but I wasn't. At the time, this short conversation with my dad seemed small and unimportant compared to the events going on around us. My life had been going pretty well, right up until my sister's murder. For me, the important questions right then were: Where would my life go from here? How would my family move forward?

Time passed, my family did move forward, and I was able to keep wrestling the center of my focus. Eventually though, I became curious about my family history, and I wanted to know more about my dad's mysterious real father.

■ ■ ■

My dad's parents were divorced, and his mother, Clemma, had remarried a Gable. My dad ended up changing his name from Leaming to Gable because of a dispute with his real father. So, by rights, I should be Dan Leaming instead of Dan Gable! To make things more confusing, the Gable family used to spell it Gabel, so there are both Gabels and Gables on that side of the family.

It turns out that my mom's side is easier to follow, but not by much. The entire time I was growing up, Gramma Lou Schnepf was around. Her partner seemed like my real grandpa, even though he wasn't. His last name was Bannon. My grandma was divorced from my real grandpa, who was a Cantwell.

It's not easy to follow, even for me. My wife is the one who is good at keeping track of these things. But the point is that they are all just names. Gable, Gabel, Leaming, Schnepf, Bannon, or Cantwell, they are all family in one way or another, and family motivates me. It turns out that I had people rooting for me whom I didn't even know. I hope I have made them all proud.

Just Normal

After the 1972 Munich Olympics, I worked for a company based out of Milwaukee, Wisconsin, called Medalist. My new main profession was the assistant wrestling coach at the University of Iowa, but Medalist signed me for a promotional contract for athletic gear and to work at their summer wrestling camps.

When you win the Olympics, sometimes business perks come along, like endorsement or promotional deals. These are a valuable asset that really help in a sport like wrestling. Today, the perks are considerably better since the old interpretation of the amateur rules is gone. Prior to 1972, the United States had a strict interpretation of these rules so that you could not profit from the sport and still be eligible to participate in the Olympics. In fact, in the summer of 1972, I had to return some money I made teaching at a camp just to stay eligible for the Olympics. The rest of the world had relaxed this interpretation, and immediately after the 1972 Olympics, the US Olympic Committee started following the rest of the world in their thinking on this. This gave athletes more chances to stay in the sport longer, especially in the United States.

Other things were changing as well. In the strength and conditioning business, new methods were being introduced and emphasized. One of the new training methods was from a company called Nautilus, led by Arthur Jones. I had already been using some of Jones's principles for lifting for years. A high school friend of mine,

Steve Tullis, got this new method from a muscle magazine, and the process was mostly about the way you returned weights to the starting position. Basically, you explode out on the positive part of the lift, and slowly return to the starting position on the negative part. In addition, my high school wrestling coach Bob Siddens always had me do maximum reps—and then five more. You had to have a partner helping, but that was just one more step to building a strong team. I learned early that "maximum" is not a fixed number.

So in the summer of 1976, four years after I won the Olympics, I was twenty-seven years old and working at a wrestling camp for Medalist in Florida. I worked technique in the morning for two hours, and then for another two hours in the early afternoon. After that second session, I challenged the kids (or they challenged me), most of whom were in high school, to takedowns. About one hundred of the three hundred kids there took me up on the challenge. So for another hour, I had to take down one hundred campers.

After I was done with all of that, I drove to meet Arthur Jones at the Nautilus site, which was close by. On the way to meet him, I stopped and got a Mountain Dew to pep me up after four hours of technique and another hour of combative wrestling. Of course, it wasn't fully combative, for I controlled the scoring and my opponents, but remember, there were a hundred of them!

I thought Arthur just wanted to meet me and have a conversation, but when I arrived at the Nautilus site at about 5:30 P.M., Arthur immediately wanted to put me through one of his famous workouts on the Nautilus machines. What do you do, say no, and not represent the sport of wrestling? Or do you take the challenge? Arthur took a lot of pride in showcasing his products and how effective they were. After all, it was just another workout, and I had been doing his type of exercises for twelve years.

Coming straight from camp and the one hundred takedowns, it was a good thing I had stopped for a quick recovery and a good-sized Mountain Dew. I know this is not a nutritional drink, but it worked for me.

Dr. Ellington Darden was a bodybuilder who trained with Arthur Jones for years, worked with him while he was developing the Nautilus system, and later wrote several books about strength and conditioning training, including *The New High Intensity Training*. He describes the Nautilus system and what it did to and for athletes.

"Arthur Jones liked to move people quickly between exercises. With his Nautilus machines, it usually took five to ten seconds to get out of one machine, and another five to ten seconds to strap into the next one. We had a guideline of fifteen to thirty seconds between machines.

"After three machines, most athletes would have a heart rate of 180 to 200 beats per minute, and it stayed in that range for the majority of the routine. Training in this manner not only worked your skeletal muscles, but also your heart and lungs—both maximally."

For me, it was a great workout, but I'm used to great workouts. Going through the entire series of twelve exercises certainly wasn't easy, especially since I was just running on Dew and water, and had already been coaching and wrestling most of the day.

"In all my years at Nautilus, I remember only one athlete who was able to go through an entire workout of twelve exercises without becoming nauseated the first time he tried it with Jones supervising," Darden says. "That athlete was Olympic champion wrestler Dan Gable. Gable was in peak shape when he visited in 1976. He impressed us all with his savvy.

"After the fourth exercise of a Jones workout, most athletes would be unable to stand. And those who tried a fifth exercise would usually have to stop midway and puke. After puking, it was over. No one ever continued after that.

"Wait, I take that back. Dick Butkus, the All-Pro middle linebacker for the Chicago Bears, hurled midway through his tenth exercise, a set of shoulder shrugs. Jones pitched an insult his way and Butkus slowly put the weight down, wiped his mouth on his arm, continued the shoulder shrug in good form, and finished his last two exercises. Then, he lumbered to the front door, turned, and threw Jones a couple of words to chew on, opened the door, and left.

"Gable and Butkus were a breed apart, at least in attitude, from the other champion athletes we trained."

For me, after four hours of teaching technique, another hour of live wrestling, capped with forty-five minutes of Nautilus training, I was just ready for a good dinner and bed. I was really surprised to hear that other athletes could not complete the workout. It also made me stop questioning whether I was still in my peak shape compared to when I won the Olympics in 1972. My lifestyle had definitely changed over the past four years, but I was still committed to hard work and working hard. For me, this was just another normal day!

■ ■ ■

This normal way of life has allowed me to continue working in the promotions area of the sport. With Medalist, and now with ASICS, I have worked with others in the field such as Bart Starr, Ernie Banks, and Al McGuire. In other travels, my family and I have been able to meet people like Howard Cosell, Muhammad Ali, Jimmy Carter, Gerald Ford, George W. Bush, Bill, Chelsea, and Hillary Clinton, Richard Nixon, Al Gore, Caitlin Jenner (formerly Bruce Jenner), Mike Tyson, the Gracies, Sugar Ray Leonard, John Wooden, Frank and Kathie Lee Gifford, Dick Vitale, Jesse Ventura, Reggie Jackson, Brooks Robinson, Billy Baldwin, Ashton Kutcher, Tom Arnold, Arnold Schwarzenegger, Mitt Romney, Donald Trump, Donald Rumsfeld, Rudy Giuliani, Jim Kelly, Bob Richards, John Irving, Bob Seagren, Joe Frazier, Bob Costas, and so on. I have been on *The Dating Game*, *To Tell the Truth*, and *The Dick Cavett Show*. This list could go on, and hopefully it will continue to grow, as wrestling grows and opportunities arise. But my point is that all these opportunities have developed from my goals and my dedication to wrestling. While I have met some impressive people, to me they are still just people. It's a normal life for me.

13

Truth Serum

I truly believe that for every cigarette you smoke, your life is that much shorter, and for every sauna you take, your life is that much longer.

The people who don't like saunas are generally ones who have not used them correctly and therefore have not experienced what they can really do. When properly used, saunas are highly effective at relaxing muscles and relieving pain after a hard workout, or just a hard day (or, for that matter, just any day). To find the right balance of heat and humidity, a lot depends on the individual and what works for them. It can take a little time and trial and error to find the right balance to make this happen. But above all, you need to sweat profusely in order to feel the sauna's good effects.

For example, I prefer a 170-degree Fahrenheit sauna with a few scoops of warm water over the sauna rocks, though I am fine if it's hotter. Any sauna, within reason, is better than no sauna at all, as long as it is doing what it needs to do. I enjoy the wood-burning heaters the most, but electric heaters are fine as well. The heater or stove is critical in creating the best possible experience. The room shouldn't struggle to reach the temperature you want.

There are many recent studies on the benefits of the sauna showing that it is an excellent tool for health, relaxation, and recovery after hard physical work. I would even say it is *the* tool. Even before science backed this up, though, athletes and those who care about their health already knew it.

Aside from the health benefits, I have found that my time in the sauna is the one time in the day when my body is fully relaxed, and so my mind is free to work hard to critique my life, my wrestling, my decisions, or whatever else may be weighing on me at the time. It gives me a chance to organize my life, as well as recover my body. By forcing me to slow down and actually evaluate my past and present, I can better plan my future. Many people are always on the run, going from one thing to another, and they fail to fully analyze and plan their lives, which causes undue stress.

In my experience, the sauna is the best tool in the world for training and recovery. Aside from the benefits to my personal mental and physical health, sauna time has helped immensely with my profession of coaching. Sure, the physical and mental recovery time aided my wrestlers' lives and performances on the mat. But even more important, after a certain amount of time in the sauna, answers to questions they may have been struggling with in their lives would start to flow. I call the sauna the "truth serum" that brings out what's inside. The sauna has often given my athletes the insight to resolve major issues or problems. It can help prevent problems, because the unknowns become known, and then we can address issues before they become a bigger problem.

Taking a sauna also develops friendships. The communication that happens is more of a respect and mental bonding. Friendships such as with my buddy Pat McGrath are strengthened while in recovery mode after a good workout and getting our minds focused on what to conquer next. My dad, Mack, Doug Moses, and Mike Duroe are among others who have sat in the sauna with me and our bonds strengthened.

For me, the sauna is a great way to wake up and get ready for the day, or a great way to recover and relax after exercising in the late afternoon. Since my evenings are for family time, I can better focus on them since I've already reviewed the day and planned for the next.

Not only are they a valuable part of the sport of wrestling, saunas can benefit a person's total health, both physical and mental. They have always been part of my life, and will continue to be in the future. Many thanks to Keith Raisanen, president of TyloHelo (formerly Saunatec, www.tylohelo.com), for believing in and providing this amazing recovery and refocusing tool.

And contrary to the Finnish culture, we do wear shorts in the sauna! But do whatever is most comfortable for you.

Total Confidence

Confidence can be contagious, especially when it is backed up with real success. When the proof is there, the confidence is real. When the proof is not there, it can be false confidence. It's like one's nerves: there is a nervous high, and that is real belief in one's self. Your good performances back up your belief. There is also a nervous scared, and that is false belief. Your not-so-good performances show.

From a coaching point of view, one has a kind of belief that is different from the athlete's. For example, in recruiting, the standard methods involve looking at the recruits' credentials, watching them wrestle in person, talking to them through phone calls, getting to know them and their family through home visits, talking with their coaches, and bringing them to campus. Based on past success, I had confidence that once a recruit signed with us and spent time on campus, he would be good, if not great. This type of belief is mostly based on a recruit's good attitude and his willingness to attend your school.

In this case, real belief comes from the system one has in place and its structure for proven performances. Even with good results, you should never stop analyzing your talent, along with the system. Talent, along with the right attitude, keeps you in the running for titles.

Surprisingly, I never saw several of the top performers in Iowa's program wrestle in person before they arrived on campus. I had faith and believed in what people I trusted were telling me about these wrestlers' potentials. If I had any doubts, I would personally witness their performances before they arrived, but those were exceptions, and that only happened if we were in second place. NCAA champions Randy Lewis, Lou Banach, Bill Zadick, and Brad Penrith are all examples of wrestlers whom I did not watch in person before they signed with Iowa. Confidence and belief can take a person a long way, but these guys all had talent.

Randy Lewis repaid my confidence in him by giving me confidence during a crucial moment in my coaching career. The 1980 NCAAs were held in Corvallis, Oregon, home of Oregon State University. The Hawkeyes had been blazing through the college wrestling world since 1975, winning four of the last five NCAA titles. But this season was very different in that we had completely changed the lineup from the previous season, with eight new starters. Several of our top wrestlers had graduated the year before. Three-time All-American Mike DeAnna was being treated for cancer in his forearm and was redshirting this year. Two-time All-American Scott Trizzino was on the sidelines with a knee surgery.

We'd had a pretty good year up to this point, with one loss to Cal Poly early in the season. This loss was a valuable coaching lesson for me. The night before the Cal Poly event, Iowa wrestled CSU–Bakersfield 140 miles away. In Iowa, where the terrain is somewhat flat, 140 miles can be about two hours' travel. This was not Iowa, but rather the mountains of California. We went up and down and around. I wasn't sure if we would make weigh-ins on time, so we went a little too fast to get there. We did make it, but not without some car-sickness and stopping to let some of the guys vomit. The weigh-ins were not a problem, but our wrestling was. There was a packed house, and boy did the sellout fans of Cal Poly have a good time. It was an historic event for Cal Poly as they stopped our string of consecutive dual victories, which was a record for us at the time. The lesson for me was two-fold: I should have checked the travel time, not just the miles, and secondly, we should have slowed down and arrived late, instead of getting sick.

Despite our overall solid record that year, I was a little too under-confident and seemed to question our chances at the NCAAs. I was feeling a little overwhelmed, until the first morning of the tournament when I walked over to the posted bracket sheets on the wall in the arena. I happened to be looking at the 134-pound bracket when a voice beside me caught my attention. It was Randy Lewis, Iowa's returning NCAA champion, up a weight category this season.

Randy, who was the number one seed, said, "Coach, see all the names on the top half of the bracket with me?"

I told him I did.

"Well, they are all going for third."

I didn't quite understand what he was getting at.

"And you see all the names on the bottom half of the bracket?"

I again replied that I did.

He made his point, saying, "They're all going for second."

He grinned, and then I got it. So I asked him, "Are the rest of the team thinking like you?"

He looked at me as though to say, *Why are you asking this?* and quickly replied, "They're all ready to go!"

It was just what I needed to make sure I didn't show any signs of doubt. I knew that Randy was probably our team's most confident member, but he gave me what I needed to help inspire the rest of them.

"I knew I was the number one seed, and I knew I was going to win. I was correct," Lewis says now. "Gaining confidence came from knowing I outworked everybody. I pinned forty-five guys in a row in high school, so I expected to pin everybody after that. I just kept getting better. I always thought I was going to pin everybody. I was able to wrestle at a very high pace and put people on their backs. I knew that if I wasn't in better shape than my opponents, I had the skills to beat them anyway, but I was always in better shape. The more you do the work, the more prepared you are, the better chance you're going to have to win—and know you're going to win."

It would be a mistake to underestimate the power of Randy's comments about everyone else on that bracket. To look at a bracket of forty outstanding wrestlers and say that, in reality, they were all going for second or third place, and that there was only one name, your own, really going for first, that is total confidence.

The team came through with an outstanding performance of two firsts (Randy, of course, at 134 pounds and Ed Banach at 177 pounds), a second (Dan Glenn at 118 pounds), two thirds (King Mueller at 150 pounds and Dean Phinney at heavyweight), a fourth (Lennie Zalesky at 142 pounds), a seventh (Mark Stevenson at 158 pounds), and an eighth (Doug Anderson at 167 pounds). That's eight All-Americans, six of whom were newcomers to the team.

Lewis's attitude gave me the jolt I needed for our team to pull off that kind of performance. The coach, the leader of the team, needs to reflect the team's performance—and boy, did we perform!

Fan Favorites

I've already talked about the toughest, the smartest, and the hardest working wrestlers, and of course these are all debatable. Another category of interest because of how entertaining and popular they are is the fan favorite.

Of course, those who dominate the mats are fan favorites, but what I'm talking about here is something different, more along the lines of the interesting characters whom the fans love both on and off the mat. The characters the media picks up on for elements besides just their wrestling. The three who immediately come to my mind are Mike DeAnna, Rico Chiapparelli, and Ray Brinzer.

■ ■ ■

Mike DeAnna, from Bay Village, Ohio, a suburb of Cleveland, was a fan favorite and one of my first big-time recruits in my initial year as head coach during the 1976–77 season. By this point, the University of Iowa had won two NCAA team titles, in 1975 and 1976, so recruits, their coaches, and their families had Iowa on their radars. Mike committed to Iowa and was good enough to not need a redshirt year his freshman year to help adjust to the higher level of college wrestling.

To help keep the team in contention for another title, Mike worked his way into the starting lineup. We already had plenty of excitement in that lineup, but Mike added an element that our fans hadn't witnessed yet: tough, offensive matches that would ignite the crowd early in the match and keep them energized right to the end. Mike often started with one or two fireman's carries that sent his opponent into orbit and would finish with snap go-behinds that would end and win the match. Some of Mike's matches would be over quickly, but when they came down to the end, Mike would send the Field House into a frenzy with his finishing moves. He kept the crowd oohing and aahing from the start to the finish.

"It was pretty amazing, because in the old Field House, you had the upper and lower deck, and everyone was really, truly matside," remembers DeAnna. "They were really close and, of course, really loud and very supportive. It was easy to feed off the enthusiasm of the fans. It was one-on-one with an opponent, and the crowd was really into it.

"The fireman's carry was something I learned when I was younger and I brought to college. I was just having a good time wrestling. That's what it was all about. It was a lot of fun to be in Iowa City where sellout crowds for wrestling were relatively new. Wrestling was fresh. It was different. It was crazy."

Aside from his entertaining wrestling, Mike's fun-loving personality made him very well liked around campus. He was a little homesick at first, which is pretty normal, but once he settled in and started hitting flashy moves, he was here at Iowa to stay.

One time though, Mike's homesickness got the better of him, and he decided he needed to go home during the coldest part of winter and set off hitchhiking to Cleveland. He made it to the border of Iowa and Illinois, about sixty miles east of Iowa City, when he turned around. It's a good thing, too, because he would have ended up a snowman if he hadn't!

Today, Mike travels to many of Iowa's dual meets. He married a good Iowa girl, Pam Anderson from Winterset, Iowa, whom he met through wrestling. Years later, they sent their daughter, Alyssa, to the University of Iowa, where she helped with the wrestling program. And now when Mike travels in the cold of winter, instead of using his thumb, he puts both hands on the steering wheel. It's much more enjoyable, I'm sure.

Mike ended his career at Iowa as a four-time Big Ten champion and a four-time All-American, reaching the finals of the NCAA wrestling tournament in 1979 and 1981.

■ ■ ■

Rico Chiapparelli, coming out of Baltimore, Maryland, wrestled at Mount St. Joe's and Blair Academy his senior year and won high school titles before enrolling at the University of Iowa. Right out of the gate, he put on the Iowa uniform with no redshirt year, and in the first month of the season, he pinned all his opponents. Then he lost, because there was something missing technically that he needed to excel at this level. That something missing was a strong leg shot to score, and some additional physical prowess that is needed for these higher levels of competition. With Royce Alger in the same room, this was not a problem, for Royce liked the weight room, ropes, and the chin-up bar, and the two of them would feed off each other.

Unlike Royce though, some of Rico's best flurries were off opponents' positions, where he would turn those around to his advantage after giving them something to work with. These kinds of moves usually brought the house to their feet, for what looked dangerous to most was Rico's way. Often, this would end in a pin for Rico. But when he was going up against really good wrestlers, this style was an issue, because giving good wrestlers any good position could mean trouble. So Rico and I had to have a powwow to make this kind of wrestling effective for both of us. Basically, he needed to learn to score more offensively. If and when his opponent really got to him, to let it happen, but only then. Then, it's all set up perfectly, it works, and he scores.

With Rico, I needed more than a handshake agreement on this; I needed a signed contract. Of course, I didn't get that either.

But instead, his dad Jerry moved to town, and his brother Louie decided to transfer and join the Hawkeyes, so now we had three Chiapparellis. I thought Rico was enough, but it all worked out fine eventually. This was important for Rico, and it helped him settle down, as he really needed people around who knew him well. His brother Louie was a little wild at first, but this move eventually helped him settle down as well. Their dad, Jerry, was not an issue, as his main goal was caring for his kids.

The crowd loved Rico and so did the ladies. That really fired Rico up, but he wouldn't admit or show it. Once you got to know him, you could tell what he enjoyed, even though he didn't show lots of emotion. He was unique, a fan favorite, and announcer Phil Haddy called him the Baltimore Butcher. The crowd loved it.

At the 1987 NCAA finals in College Park, Maryland, Rico scored on the edge of the mat with a single shot for crucial points early. It was a tough match, and his opponent, Darryl Pope of Cal State–Bakersfield, went in on him for a winning shot late in the match. There was a flurry of action and twenty or thirty seconds of counter-wrestling on both sides before Rico ended up on top for the take-down. Those twenty to thirty seconds were some of the wildest and most nervous of my wrestling life, but Rico came out of it a champion.

That victory went all the way back to his freshman year. Rico was a much more complete wrestler in 1987, but the tools he came in with won that match for him. Some programs would have taken his best from him because of the risk, but not Iowa, and he came out a winner because of it.

That wild finish at the 1987 NCAAs reminds me of another wild finish for another Iowa wrestler: Randy Lewis versus a Russian opponent during an international dual meet at Arizona State. The moment was the same: twenty to thirty seconds of wild counters at the finish, and Randy ended up on top. It made for thunderous applause and excitement and was a great promotion for the sport of wrestling. From east to west, Iowa wrestling has excitement and influence.

Rico was a three-time All-American at Iowa, placing fifth at the 1985 NCAA wrestling tournament, fourth in 1986, and first in 1987, all at 177 pounds. He currently works with wrestling through mixed martial arts.

■ ■ ■

Another fan favorite was Ray Brinzer of Pittsburgh, Pennsylvania, from Gus DeAugustino's famous program at North Allegheny High School. Ray initially went to Oklahoma State, wrestled there for one year, then transferred to the University of Iowa. He ended up living in the parking lot of Carver-Hawkeye Arena as a team walk-on with no scholarship and very little money.

"I managed to string together enough money to pay my tuition, but not to pay rent or for food," remembers Brinzer. "All I had was tuition money, so I paid my tuition. I had a truck and I had a futon. I got some crates and put my stuff underneath the crates, like a loading pallet, and I put the futon on top of it. And I slept under the topper in the back of the truck because I couldn't afford to live anywhere. Nobody was allowed to help me because I was an athlete. If they helped me, it would be an NCAA violation.

"I just rode out that semester out of determination. If I can make it to Christmas, then I get my scholarship back, and I can live inside again. At some point, I bought this enormous thing of ramen noodles, because it's never bad to have staple food because I'll always have this. I basically ended up living on it for the semester. There was an apple tree outside the nursing building. A significant part of my diet was eating from that apple tree.

"I would show up with a pair of pants with knots tied around in the legs, climb the tree with the pants wrapped around my neck, and pick apples. So I would have apples and ramen. At various times, I would try to find a place to sleep indoors, because it gets very, very cold. Occasionally I'd sneak into Carver-Hawkeye Arena and sleep in Royce Alger's office, but I got thrown out of there a couple times. I was able to sleep there a number of nights before I got caught and basically threatened."

I didn't know about any of this and thought Ray looked good, until one morning a month into fall, when I arrived at Carver early in the morning and saw his pick-up truck parked in a back corner spot near the woods. I walked over to his truck and looked inside. Ray was asleep on a small mattress on the bottom of the truck bed. I knocked on the window, woke him up, and we talked. This is when I found out he had not moved in with anybody.

I asked him, "This is where you sleep?"

"Yes."

"Where do you eat?"

"At a local soup kitchen."

"What?" Walk-on or not, the thought of one of my athletes eating at the local soup kitchen shocked me.

"Yes. Also, it's been getting cold at nights, and I might need to get more blankets."

"Okay, enough is enough," I told him. "We need to talk and get this figured out!"

Ray had been at Oklahoma State for a year, and he didn't know about Iowa's cold days and nights. Plus, he was an athlete, as well as a student, so nutrition was especially important. After this, the wrestling team helped him find temporary indoor housing with someone who had the space for a roommate.

I also asked Ray about his schooling. He told me he was having difficulties in one of his classes. When I asked him why, he said,

"Well, I'm doing fine in all the exams and the tests. But this class, the professor wants homework and actual attendance in class. In fact, it's required, otherwise I flunk."

"You're not going to classes?"

"No, except for test days," he said. "Homework and attendance are for those who don't understand. I understand. I'm getting all As and Bs on the tests."

I could see Ray's point, but that attitude was clearly not going to work if he wanted to pass and become eligible to wrestle as a Hawkeye.

"There was a lot of stuff about college I didn't get," Brinzer says now. "I didn't really understand the entire thing. I paid very little attention to it before I got there."

We had quite a lengthy conversation about the importance of classroom attendance, with me explaining that he needed professor time with all the instructors who had this policy so he could pass and wrestle. Ray was really good at intellectual conversations like this, and he finally got on board with this policy. I'm not sure if he actually stuck with regular classroom attendance and doing homework, but his grades were good enough that he was eligible to wrestle.

Getting Ray to practice on time was another issue though. He always intended to be on time, but as he became more well known around campus, students and teachers would stop him to talk. These conversations went beyond basic greetings, and they were always interesting and long. So I had to put a system in place to make sure Ray didn't get distracted and miss practice: I assigned another wrestler to get him to practice on time. I knew he wasn't doing it on purpose, but we had to stay after practice more than a few times to catch him up on what he missed. He was good, but even Ray had to go to wrestling practice to be great.

Ray had followers of his own, in addition to the regular Iowa wrestling fans. He liked to wear tie-dyed t-shirts and Elton John glasses, and those are what his fan club tended to wear as well. They would sit together at meets in their shirts and glasses and cheer him on especially loudly. After all, Ray's wrestling was unique and fun to watch.

"It felt like I had friends and I had a new hometown," says Ray. "Being at Iowa was good for me socially. As far as the intensity of being watched and being adored, I got tired of that. By the time I was done there, I was ready to be out of the spotlight. I like it much better on the personal level. I like having fans whom I talk to, and we have a normal conversation. It was connecting with people. That's part of why they liked me, because I never felt like I was better than them.

"When they took an interest in me, I took an interest in them. When kids wanted to talk or get an autograph, I always gave it. I had matches my senior year [1995] at nationals in Iowa City, where I would come off the mat, and kids would approach me for autographs, and I would sign autographs continuously until my next match. And that's fine. I didn't need to prepare for my next match. I knew what I was going to do. I was giving back something to somebody. It's nice to make some kind of difference."

Another unique thing about Ray was that he had a little voodoo doll he would set in the coaches' corner of the mat during matches. Whether a coach was there or not, his doll was in his corner. It would just sit there, staring at Ray. It seemed to work, so we let him keep it.

Ray was a two-time All-American, placing third at the NCAA wrestling tournament in 1993 and 1995 at 177 pounds. He is currently a computer programmer who most recently coached wrestling for Beat the Streets in New York City. His favorite coaching title was assistant junior high wrestling coach.

16

Know Your Limit

I've never been a big-time beer drinker. I've been around it quite a bit, especially with all the celebrating I've gotten to do over the years, but it just wasn't conducive for what I've wanted to accomplish in my life. Not only would it do too much damage to my training and my coaching, but potentially also to what is really important: my family. My parents drank a bit too much when I was a kid, and sometimes it could lead to shouting and even violence. I never wanted that for my own family.

In the spring of 1986, the Iowa Hawkeyes were celebrating our ninth straight NCAA championship title. That tied the record for championship streaks in any NCAA sport. Not long after, the athletic department asked the head basketball coach, George Raveling, and me to be the cooks for a local boosters' event. All we had to do was flip burgers over a big grill for an hour or two. We were working pretty hard though because it was a big crowd, and the big grill was plenty hot. But the crowd made sure we constantly had the drinks we wanted. That was fine, but at the end of the event, a couple of Iowa backers wanted me to go downtown with them. I obliged. What could I say, no? But almost as soon as I walked in the door of the bar, someone brought me a mixed drink. Then another.

I knew I needed to head home, as I had an early morning fishing trip planned with Lloyd Bender. Lloyd was a photographer for the University of Iowa Photographic Services, and a very good fisherman. We were planning on heading to the local reservoir and fishing for bass.

Upon arriving home, I was quite dizzy and made the wise decision to sleep on the couch so I wouldn't disturb Kathy when I got up early in the morning. But early morning came too soon, and I was in no shape to get up and go fishing. I went anyway though, and was totally miserable. I tried to hide it; I guess I was too proud to show weakness, even to my friend.

Lloyd was in the front of the boat, both fishing and running the trolling motor. The fish were really biting up there, and he was catching plenty. I was in the back of the boat, where I was doing a poor job of hiding my hangover. Add in the fact that we were casting toward the shoreline, and I had no accuracy since I was feeling pretty sick, so I would either land on the rocks or ten feet from the shoreline in the water. It's no surprise that I caught no fish.

After a few hours, I barely got down a Mountain Dew and started to feel better. When I got home in the late morning, I told my wife that I would never again drink to excess. I vowed to never have more than two beers in a day.

I am proud to say that, more than thirty years later, I have kept that vow. It might be one of the single greatest accomplishments of my life. I know it has kept my family together and allowed me to continue to achieve more in my wrestling profession. There is no telling how much influence it has had on the many people who know me or follow me. I don't know where I'd be right now without this pact between me and my limits, but thanks to it, I'm still achieving my goals and striving for new accomplishments.

After all, people are only as good as their word!

The Smartness of Hard Work

I should have been smarter.

That's the best way I can describe what happened in 1987. We knew what was supposed to happen that year: just like the nine previous seasons, the Iowa Hawkeyes were going to win a national championship. Our teams had been tearing up the college wrestling world for over a decade, and 1987 was going to be the year we would win our tenth consecutive NCAA team championship. I knew it, the team knew it, and the rest of the wrestling world knew it. Or so I thought.

We were so confident that we would win this tenth consecutive championship that we had the Roman numeral X stitched on the leg of our uniforms. That was the goal, and that was the plan. Winning that tenth championship would have been a record performance. No collegiate team had ever done it in any sport at that point.

Our championship streak had begun ten years earlier at the 1978 NCAA wrestling tournament in College Park, Maryland, when I was in my second season as the head wrestling coach. We had placed third in 1977, my rookie season as head coach, and we were poised to make a run the following year.

Going into the 1978 championship finals, Iowa led 94.5 to 89.5, with two individual finalists. Randy Lewis, a true freshman who was seeded second at 126 pounds, faced Iowa State's top-seeded and un-defeated Mike Land. Lewis had lost to him three times during the season. Land won again here, and Iowa State narrowed the gap to 94.5 to 94.

But our team had another opportunity to score points at 150 pounds when our third-seeded wrestler, Bruce Kinseth, faced off against Michigan's top-seeded Mark Churella. Kinseth lost that match, so we kept the same number of points and still held a razor-thin lead of half a point.

Earlier in the tournament, Oklahoma State's radio commentator, J. Carl Guymon, caught a scoring error that had given Iowa State an extra team point in an early round. Officials corrected the mis-take, and Hawkeye fans still remember Guymon's contribution to our program.

Iowa State still had one more chance to beat us though. Cyclone senior Frank Santana, the defending NCAA champion, was wres-tling Wisconsin's Ron Jeidy. Santana was the top-seeded wrestler at 190 pounds, and he had defeated Jeidy twice in the season. If San-tana won now, it would give Iowa State enough team points to beat us for the team championship.

"I think all of us dream of having the team win come down to you, the big match, the big tournament—and it doesn't get any big-ger than the NCAA championships," remembers Santana. "I was looking forward to the fact that it was going to come down to me. I was the last chance for us to win."

Jeidy held a 3–1 lead in the second period, and Santana was fight-ing off a shot. During the action, there was a loud pop in Santana's right knee. He later found out that he tore his ACL. Santana con-tinued wrestling, but his knee became so bad that Harold Nichols, Iowa State's head wrestling coach and my college coach, threw in the towel, signifying the end of the match. This gave the University of Iowa the first NCAA team title with me as the head wrestling coach.

"That match was the greatest disappointment that a young athlete can have, to let his teammates down and not be able to deliver," says Santana now. "It was something that I struggled with for many months and many years after."

I don't believe in luck for the most part, but at that point the championship was outside our control. Two other athletes from different teams decided our fate, and for the defending national champion to lose with my college coach throwing in the towel, that's really rare. How could anyone have called that finish?

So Iowa's dominance began after we escaped with a half-point victory in 1978. Our average margin of victory over second place for the next eight seasons was just over 38 points. Our closest team race was in 1982, and even then, we still won by 20.75 points.

In 1986, we had our most dominant championship, crowning five NCAA champions, eight All-Americans, and scoring a then-record 158 points. Runner-up Oklahoma scored 84.75 points, which was 73.25 points behind us.

So when we failed to win that tenth title in 1987, anyone watching the world of college wrestling was shocked. Interestingly, it happened again in College Park, Maryland, the same place where it all started. When the smoke cleared at the fifty-seventh NCAA wrestling championships, it was the Iowa State Cyclones, led by second-year head wrestling coach Jim Gibbons, winning the title and, in doing so, crushing our dreams and those of our fans. Iowa State blasted the competition with 133 points and four NCAA champions. We were a disappointing second with 108 points.

"We were the mentally stronger team at that point, and we executed under pressure," says Gibbons. "I'm amazed today, and everyone else from that team gets the same feeling, at how continually rewarding winning the 1987 NCAA tournament was. It was great when it happened, and nothing can replace that Iowa State was the team that stopped the streak that Dan had. What Iowa was able to do during that streak was magnificent."

We had planned a rare family celebration trip to Hawaii immediately after the NCAAs. It was going to be a wonderful way to celebrate that tenth national title. With a defeat in my lap and tickets and hotel accommodations already paid for, we still went to the islands. There was no celebrating, but something occurred that paved the way for our wrestling program to move forward, and for me personally.

We had been there for about a day, and I was miserable, when Kathy finally said, "This isn't working. You need to take some time and go off and deal with this loss."

Kathy was right and I knew it. So each day, as the rest of the family headed out in the morning, I stayed behind in the hotel room and analyzed what had gone wrong and how we didn't win that record-setting team championship. Overlooking the ocean, I started to make notes about where we were as a program and how we could get it back to where we needed to be. I was studying the past so I could better plan for the future. With time to focus each morning, I was able to enjoy the remaining hours of the day with my family. The trip lasted a week, but the ideas I put in place there are still evolving to this day.

I allowed my mind to open so I could analyze my life and the Iowa wrestling program. I had to better understand how the program had gone from where we were to where we had just landed. The answers were there, and as painful as some parts of my personal and program audit were, I took notes so I could implement the necessary personal and professional changes.

From that time forward, I took a working vacation every year after the NCAA championships. While on these trips, I evaluated the previous season and planned for the next, often planning well beyond the next season. It was a time to go over what we had done as a team and as individuals and to start putting together the plan for the next season. Even more important though, these trips gave me time away from the wrestling office to relax and recover. I could have stayed home and worked out of my house, but that would not have worked because of the closeness of the "pull" of my normal life and habits. The distance and the attractions made the difference. The real help was my family knowing how to make it all work.

■ ■ ■

When you are in a position of authority, you sometimes make mistakes. That's what happened here: I made mistakes. We had built our program on the ideals of hard work, discipline, and outworking everyone else. We did this by being more dedicated and more disciplined, not just in wrestling, but in all areas of life.

Discipline in one area of your life helps, but the more, the better. Any parts of life that are not disciplined will leave openings for vulnerabilities. This can be difficult, but any vices should be kept to a minimum and under control.

I never agreed with the wrestlers who argued they could be even better if they "just didn't have to go to class." They believed they could be better wrestlers if they could be full-time wrestlers. I completely disagree with that notion. It doesn't work, not even on the Olympic level. People will say it does, but it doesn't. Having other important parts of life that complement wrestling is not only good, but also vital to helping an athlete prepare for training. It's called recovery.

That time away from the wrestling room, weight room, or track is part of the daily recovery process, physically and mentally. Recovery time needs to be filled with good things, like going to class, studying, spending time with family and friends, or hobbies.

I realized that I was not allowing myself time to recover. I was not doing the very thing I was adamant about with my wrestlers. When we were winning Big Ten titles and national championships, I would celebrate on Saturday night after the tournament, take Sunday mostly off, and then be back in the office working on Monday. Functioning this way is not smart, and it took this loss and stern words from my wife for me to figure it out.

A baffling aspect of this second-place finish was that it was by a team of wrestlers much more heralded than previous teams. In my early years at Iowa, we didn't have the highest-ranked recruiting classes. Wrestlers came into our system of discipline, hard work, and focus, and that formula led to the NCAA titles in those early years. We won because of our relentless style of wrestling and training.

With this system of hard work and discipline in place, a dynasty had been created. Then, in 1982, we got the number one recruiting class in the country.

In hindsight, I realized that that was when the Iowa work ethic began to slip. In many ways, winning came almost too easy for these freshmen as they trampled their way to the NCAA team championship in 1983. In doing so, the seeds of collapse were planted.

This class was so talented that they could get away with a little less discipline in and out of the wrestling room than some of the previous classes. They weren't doing anything terrible, but we were not fully living up to the hard work ethic that had built us into a great program.

Now that I look back at it, with the talent I had on that roster (Alger, Penrith, the Chiapparellis, the Randalls), my job became more about managing their lives off the mat than being their wrestling coach. They were good people, but I had to help them keep their lives in order. I could turn them loose on the mat, but away from the mat, these guys needed to be reeled in more than I was doing.

The recruiting classes from 1984 through 1986 were talented, but not as talented as the recruiting classes from 1982 and 1983. Those incoming wrestlers saw what the wrestlers ahead of them were doing and not doing, so the work ethic and attitude slipped a little more. Winning had become too easy.

We were celebrating all those NCAA championships and Big Ten titles instead of focusing on the next season. We assumed the next championship would happen automatically—and nothing is ever automatic. And now, each year we were slipping a little further away from the attitude of hard work and discipline that it took to build what we had at Iowa.

This is not to say that we were not working hard, just not to the standard that we used to have, which laid the foundation of multiple championships. Also, as the discipline in the wrestling room began to wane, other, more serious, problems arose. There was more partying and less discipline in other areas of the wrestlers' lives.

In the early years of the Hawkeyes' national championship run, the wrestlers had a reputation in the community as being good young men. Problems on and off campus were rare, but as discipline in the wrestling room began to drop off, problems with a few select members of our team in the community began to increase. Where we used to be contributors to the community, our guys started fighting and causing other problems. There was too much celebrating, too many late hours, and more arrests than normal for alcohol abuse or disorderly conduct. Guys still showed up for 6:30 A.M. practices, but they were coming in after a night of partying. In that situation, I had to send them home. They needed sleep more than practice.

I admit that I saw these problems at the time, but when I should have stepped in and fixed the discipline issues, I did not. Instead, I just kept saying, "We're winning, there really are no problems." But there were problems, and not just with the athletes. The coaching staff was also becoming a little cocky, and the community was losing respect for us.

I finally started to address these issues four months prior to the NCAAs, after our dual meet loss to Penn State in State College, Pennsylvania, in December 1986. I started cracking down on discipline, but it was clearly too little, too late.

With our streak of NCAA titles over at nine in a row in 1987, I returned to Hawkeye wrestling's roots. Discipline and the concept of outworking everyone else went back into place. I made some tough decisions, changed certain positions on the coaching staff, and hired some new faces. It was all part of my plan to return the Hawks to the top of the wrestling world, while working just as hard to regain the respect in Iowa City.

I didn't hide the fact that we had fallen short. The 1988 team poster opened many eyes: it was a garbage can full of trash that we needed to clean up. It stated simply, "A New Era."

While the team took the process of taking out the trash and returning to our roots seriously, our return to the top as national champions was slow. Many anticipated an immediate turnaround. I probably felt that way too. But you have to understand what happened here; it took several years to create this problem, and it was going to take several years to fix it.

Brad Penrith, our 1986 NCAA champion at 126 pounds as a sophomore, has another view, and an interesting one at that.

"I was partly to blame, since I lost in the 1987 NCAA tournament finals," says Penrith. "There's individual performance, and there's team performance when you get down to the end. After that, Gable took recruiting more seriously. He started making more personal visits with kids after we placed second in 1987."

In many ways, Penrith is right. After 1987, I weighed in more on the type of recruits we needed, based on what was already in the room and what was missing. What we were missing were examples of extreme dedication and discipline, and because this had been missing for a few years, an immediate fix was unlikely.

This is exactly what happened. When something needs to be fixed or adjusted, the longer one waits to fix the problem, the longer it takes to get back in line. The Longer, the Longer!—four very important words to remember. They apply to almost everything.

So we kept our noses to the grindstone, setting goals and recruiting the right kinds of athletes who embraced getting the Hawkeye work ethic and discipline back into the program. While we cultivated the program back to its self-imposed standards, we didn't win any national championships. Instead, Arizona State won in 1988, followed by back-to-back championships by Oklahoma State in 1989 and 1990. Our teams placed second, second, sixth, and third during our four-year championship drought.

We finally got back to where we needed to be to win the national championship in 1991, putting to rest any thoughts the Oklahoma State Cowboys may have had of building a dynasty of their own after winning two championships in a row. We won that title with 157 points, while defending-champion Oklahoma State scored 108.75 points.

That championship was extremely rewarding, especially since it was at Carver-Hawkeye Arena. We climbed back to the top, and we had done it by being smarter than before and with the original Iowa work ethic.

After the letdown in 1987 and the four-year rebuilding project that followed, we won three championships (1991–93), placed second to Oklahoma State in 1994, and won three more titles in a row (1995–97). After my retirement in 1997, Jim Zalesky—a three-time NCAA champion for the Hawkeyes (1983–85)—led the program to three more championships (1998–2000). Current Iowa head wrestling coach and former Hawkeye wrestler Tom Brands—a three-time NCAA champion (1990–92), World champion (1993), and an Olympic gold medalist (1996)—led the Hawkeyes to NCAA championships in 2008, 2009, and 2010. Tom's first year of head coaching at Iowa was 2007. Athletic director Bob Bowlsby, who hired Tom, convinced me to come back as an assistant coach for that year.

We needed to go through what we did in 1987 in order to get better. That loss made me a better coach. Had I taken working vacations that included evaluating and planning every year, we might not have lost that 1987 NCAA tournament. Sometimes, our worst losses can be our best teachers.

18

The Missing Year-Round Plan

Iowa placed sixth at the 1989 NCAA wrestling tournament, and that didn't sit well with me. For the first and only time in my twenty-one seasons as head coach, the Hawkeyes finished without a team trophy—only given to the top four teams—after we had worked our way to the top and were one of the three teams favored to win. Oklahoma State, Arizona State, and Iowa were all favored, and on back-to-back dates in February, we won dual meets over both. Of course, both were home duals, and the NCAAs were in Oklahoma that year. We clearly weren't good enough to beat them on the road, which is always our top priority.

We didn't have any individual NCAA tournament finalists that year either, another first for Iowa since 1974. I watched the finals from press row without a representative from Iowa in any of the weight classes. After the Saturday morning wrestlebacks, we were done.

Yes, we were rebuilding the team's leadership, but after finishing second the past two years, this was a step even further back in the final team standings. Our fans could see the Hawkeyes' future possibilities, but all I was seeing were the results, and in the spring of 1989, those results weren't great. I needed to eliminate any more possible setbacks.

We had a really good recruiting class full of potential in the fall of 1987. It included lots of Iowa kids who fed off the program and off themselves. This class included Mark Reiland of Eagle Grove, Iowa; Bart Chelesvig of Webster City, Iowa; Pat Kelly of Britt, Iowa; and Tom and Terry Brands of Sheldon, Iowa. Kelly later ended up transferring out and became an All-American for the University of Nebraska–Omaha, a top Division II program no longer sponsoring the sport. It was a tough loss for the sport and especially the school when it comes to taking away notable excellence. But between the other four, they won thirteen All-American honors and six NCAA titles. The Brands brothers also became World champions and Olympic medalists, with a gold for Tom and a bronze for Terry.

So our fans could look to the future and see what we would be capable of in the coming years. Ed McGinness, one of our lead supporters, told me that between the recruits of the fall of 1987 and the Steiner twins coming in with the next class in 1988, he saw it all fitting together for the future. After placing sixth, I needed this kind of confidence, inspiration, and assurance for the future coming from beyond just the staff and athletes. It motivated me and helped with my confidence, which would spill over daily to the athletes. And McGinness and the other fans were right: after that sixth-place finish in 1989, we improved to third in 1990, and then we were back to winning NCAA championships.

But immediately after that sixth-place finish at the 1989 NCAA tournament, I knew we had to do something. We put together a comprehensive document that laid out the entire plan for the coming year—or any year—on paper. I had one copy that everyone—team members, coaches, assistants—had to read, study, and sign. They had to read it in my office while I was present, though they could come back for a second or third reading if they wanted. Make no mistake, I needed everybody to understand the system going forward. None of this, "No, Coach, I didn't understand or get it." There were now no excuses for a misunderstanding. Even though the future looked good, I go more on actual results.

The document outlined a 365-day plan for success in winning the NCAA wrestling championships. It started with the day after the Saturday night of the NCAA finals. This was Day 1 of Phase 1, which was the Recovering, Evaluating, and Planning Phase. It included my working vacation and lasted about seven to fourteen days. There were about fourteen phases total, ending with Saturday night of the NCAAs, ten individual champions, and a first-place team finish. This plan worked, because Iowa went on to win the NCAA championships again in 1991, 1992, 1993, 1995, 1996, 1997, 1998, 1999, 2000, 2007, 2008, and 2009.

At some point over the years, this original hardcopy plan was lost, which is a pity. With so many successful wrestlers and coaches signing it, sometimes more than once, it is fairly historic. I don't know if it was stolen or lost or just misplaced. There are rumors about what happened to it, one of which is that Tom Brands borrowed it, and then Tom Ryan from Ohio State borrowed it from him. I don't really believe that though.

I've been asked to reconstruct this 365-day plan for wrestling coaches at all levels, as well as the athletes themselves and even business leaders. I could probably do it again, since all the information is still there in my brain, but it won't be the same, as times have changed and the sport has continued to evolve. But if I do reconstruct it someday, I'm not trusting anyone with only one copy. I've learned my lesson!

We should all have a 365-day yearly plan, and putting it down on paper not only helps you, it also gets that information out in front of you and your team, which is critical for performance and understanding. Teams need to be on the same page as their leader. Work together, win together. Share the message. And always keep a backup.

19

Sign of the Times

When Gary Kurdelmeier became the new head wrestling coach at the University of Iowa in the fall of 1972, he had a vision of what the Hawkeye wrestling program could be. Gary is from Cresco, Iowa, home of the Iowa Wrestling Hall of Fame, as well as many big names in the sport, including my college wrestling coach Harold Nichols and the wrestler I patterned my original style after, Tom Peckham. The most famous Cresco wrestler is Nobel Peace Prize–winner Norman Borlaug, a plant biologist who helped farmers worldwide increase production and cut down on global hunger. I'm proud to be included in a mural on a building in Cresco, Iowa, that portrays several famous locals, all of whom wrestled.

Gary Kurdelmeier (the architect) wanted to make Iowa one of the top wrestling programs in the nation, and his plan to get there was simple: get multimillionaire Roy Carver from Muscatine involved with the wrestling program and start the Hawkeye Wrestling Club for post-graduates to be able to train for the Olympics with the Hawkeye team. Next, get me to be his assistant coach. With Gary's guidance, this all became a reality.

Gary's promotional skills were phenomenal. He was constantly coming up with ways of making wrestling an event that people wanted to attend. He found an organ and someone to play it during meets. It drove the other team crazy, but the crowds thought it was fun. For the meet against Oklahoma, he put together that huge seventy-four by seventy-four foot mat. Leading up to that meet, he promoted it as "The World's Largest Wrestling Mat." We didn't get to keep the big mat, of course, but we got something more important for the sport and the team: larger audiences.

Another promotional tool Gary created was the poster schedule for the upcoming season. These were unique, and each year was theme-based, depending on what was currently going on with the team and in popular culture. The posters were placed in businesses throughout the community and elsewhere. In the beginning, they mostly just promoted the program and the events. But as individual wrestlers gained recognition, the content changed. We started putting returning All-Americans on the posters. The designs became flashier, and people noticed the posters more and more. Many are worth mentioning, but here are just a few of my favorites.

Going into the 1985 season, after winning seven NCAA champion-ships in a row and nine out of the last ten, as well as eleven straight Big Ten championships, we were seen as the villains in college wres-tling. We were winning too much for the rest of the country and not sharing all those championship titles. We were starting to get new fans from all over because people liked our dominant style of wres-tling. At that point, you either liked us, or you hated us! We decided to use exactly that in that year's promotional schedule.

Back then, one of the most popular shows on television was *Dallas*. It was a show loaded with drama about a large and powerful family, led by J. R. Ewing. This was the inspiration for the promotional poster. It showed me sitting there in my office, directing the All-Americans on to big things. It was a little unusual for me, given my humble be-ginnings and natural shyness, but if you've got it, sometimes you have to flaunt it. And we certainly had it going at this point!

The next season, 1986, we were still flaunting our success a little on the poster, for in small letters we claimed our record would grow to "nine in a row." This goal didn't come without a setback, for we were upset in our last dual of the year at Iowa State. That was the only major flaw of the year though, and we came back a month later to win our ninth straight national title, with five individual champions, one second-place finish, and two other All-Americans.

By 1987, we thought we were set to win our tenth consecutive national championship, and we weren't shy about it. We put the Roman numeral X everywhere: on the new poster schedule, t-shirts, hats, bumper stickers, even stitched right into the leg of our uniforms! What was I thinking? I wasn't. I was just too confident that nine would become ten, just like how one became two, two became three, and so on. With all those bragging Xs out there, we should have been tough enough to back it up. But we weren't tough enough in our discipline, and so we failed to get that record tenth national title, and finished in second place.

After our second-place finish the previous year, we knew we needed to clean house and make some changes in 1988. Our poster schedule reflected that; it was quite different from our past in-your-face flaunting. Labeled "A New Era," it showed a lot of the changes that were already taking place. As the coach, I needed to exert more control over the wrestlers, encouraging hard work and discipline, and making sure that there were consequences for bad behavior. The athletes needed to work to gain back the community's respect. The poster for this season showed all the garbage that was coming from our program being hauled to the dump. It was quite a change in perspective, and it needed to be done. We were able to turn things around, slowly but surely, and effect positive changes throughout the program.

Going into the 1992 season, we were loaded at every weight: we had a whole team—plus one—of All-Americans and NCAA champions. This group was full of positive influences, and they helped sway the entire team. I love comparing the 1992 team with the teams of 1983 and 1997.

20

Big Ten Streak

Greatness is built on crucial decisions made at crucial times. The 1992–93 season proved to be one of those times, one that could have altered the course of my coaching career.

That year, Iowa only brought back four starters from the previous two seasons, which meant that we had to prove ourselves to the outside world all over again. The larger wrestling community knew that we replaced studs with studs, but replacing 60 percent of the team gave hope to our opponents. In addition, a new school with an excellent wrestling team entered the Big Ten conference that year: Penn State. Iowa's only loss under me at Carver-Hawkeye Arena was to Penn State, 19–18 (pre Big 10 conference). That sort of thing really sticks with you—especially when your lifetime record at Carver-Hawkeye Arena is 98–1, with three NCAA titles and two Big Ten titles earned there.

The Hawkeyes had won every Big Ten tournament dating back to 1974 when Gary Kurdelmeier was the coach, a string of nineteen in a row entering the 1993 season. When you have a streak going you obviously don't want to stop. But when Penn State came into the conference, they were looking to stop us. In order to win our twentieth Big Ten title, we had to pull out all the stops.

One step was to pull a promising young freshman out of redshirt status late in the season. Lincoln McIlravy, a five-time state champion from Philip, South Dakota, wrestled at 142 pounds. This meant that someone would have to move out of the way to make room for him in the lineup. That someone was defending 142-pound NCAA champion Troy Steiner.

Steiner's willingness to make this move began the previous summer.

"We graduated six starters from the team the year before," he remembers. "There was a guy in a wheelchair during summer wrestling camp. I was waiting to cross the street with him, and he said, 'How are you guys looking?' I told him we were looking pretty good, and he told me that we weren't going to do it this year because we lost too much. It hit me like, 'We're going to do this again, and we're going to win again.'"

That passion and belief are what led him to move down a weight class for the good of the team.

"I was really excited to come out of redshirt," says McIlravy. "I wasn't aware of the Big Ten streak at all, to be honest. The expectation at Iowa was to put the best team on the mat that they could, regardless of any statistical history that was on the line. I think Coach Gable and the rest of the staff were really good about allowing the athletes to focus on the things they actually had control over, not the last fifteen years, not a team title, but just the best individual contribution to the team."

So with Troy willing to move down, and Lincoln feeling ready to step into his place, I felt that the 142-pound and the 134-pound spots were in good hands.

Another question mark was at 126 pounds. Our 126-pounder was big for the weight class and had trouble making the weight a couple of times during the season, so I had a second wrestler ready to go at the Big Ten tournament just in case. I don't think most programs have two guys ready to go, but it was important for us in these circumstances. When we found out that our 126-pounder didn't make the weight class, all we had to do was open another door at the hotel, and there was Kevin Hogan, ready and waiting.

There was one final surprise waiting for us at the Big Ten tournament—and no one saw it coming.

A very good wrestler named Ray Brinzer had transferred from Oklahoma State to Iowa at the start of the year. Brinzer's eligibility during his transfer was unclear, so he did not get to wrestle for Iowa during the season. He did compete in a couple of open tournaments during the season, and he also trained at Foxcatcher Farm in Newtown Square, Pennsylvania, over the winter break to keep in shape. The NCAA gave Brinzer permission to wrestle for us just as the Hawkeyes were heading to the Big Ten tournament. Thus, the Hawkeyes' newest 177-pounder entered the Big Ten tournament with a 0–0 record.

Because of his non-record, Ray was unseeded, and the luck of the draw matched him with the number one seed in the first match. This happened to be Penn State's Matt White, Ray's former high school teammate at North Allegheny High School in Pittsburgh, Pennsylvania, who was a year ahead of Brinzer and in high school had wrestled a weight class up.

"Nobody outside Iowa and Oklahoma State knew I was there until I weighed in that morning," said Brinzer. "Matt wasn't too happy to see me."

All of our late season moves ended up paying off. We had two Big Ten champions, Chad Zaputil (118) and Troy Steiner (134). McIlravy placed second to Wisconsin's Dan Spilde at 142 pounds. Brinzer also placed second, including an opening round win over White. Troy's brother, Terry, also placed second, as did Joel Sharratt at 190 pounds.

Terry Steiner and Lincoln McIlravy went on to win individual NCAA tournament titles that year. McIlravy won a thrilling 16–15 come-from-behind match over Gerry Abas of Fresno State in the finals. Steiner won 8–7 on a last-second takedown over Penn State's Troy Sunderland, a rematch of the Big Ten finals.

But it was Kevin Hogan, our hideout 126-pounder, who made the ultimate difference for us in keeping our Big Ten streak alive. Without Hogan's 5.5 points and fifth-place finish, we would have lost by one point. He has a special place in my heart for that reason, among others.

With that, we won our twentieth Big Ten tournament in a row and my seventeenth as the head coach. It helped make legends of many of my wrestlers. We followed that up with another dominant NCAA championship performance in Ames, Iowa, where we beat Penn State with a 123.75 to 87.5 win.

Iowa's twentieth straight Big Ten title in 1993 tied Indiana University's string of twenty straight swimming titles coached by the late great James "Doc" Cousilman from 1961 to 1980. What team stopped Indiana swimming's Big Ten conference streak in 1981? It was none other than the Iowa Hawkeyes and Coach Glen Patton. Thanks, Glen.

During my twenty-one seasons as head wrestling coach, the Hawkeyes won twenty-one consecutive Big Ten titles. I still like how that feels. There are more than enough 1s on the losing side that drive me batty: 181–1 in high school and college (I lost to Larry Owings in the 1970 NCAA tournament finals), 9–1 NCAA consecutive team titles (we lost to Iowa State at the 1987 NCAA wrestling tournament), 98–1 dual meet record at Carver-Hawkeye Arena (we lost to Penn State in 1988). Of course, if we had won them all, they all would have been record performances, but learning from the losses to get better is what really counts.

Even better than twenty-one out of twenty-one Big Ten titles is twenty-five out of twenty-five when you include Kurdelmeier before me, and Zalesky after me. Below is a list of our streak of twenty-five

Big Ten titles in a row, along with Iowa's points, the runner-up team with their points, and the host city of the Big Ten wrestling tournament.

1974 (Kurdelmeier), Iowa 151, Michigan 123
  at Evanston, Illinois
1975 (Kurdelmeier), Iowa 118.5, Wisconsin 85.5
  at Columbus, Ohio
1976 (Kurdelmeier), Iowa 97.25, Minnesota 57.5
  at Iowa City, Iowa
1977 (Gable), Iowa 107.75, Minnesota 65.5
  at Madison, Wisconsin
1978 (Gable), Iowa 117.25, Wisconsin 94
  at Ann Arbor, Michigan
1979 (Gable), Iowa 106.25, Wisconsin 90.5
  at Iowa City, Iowa
1980 (Gable), Iowa 99.75, Wisconsin 80.75
  at East Lansing, Michigan
1981 (Gable), Iowa 126.75, Minnesota 57.5
  at Madison, Wisconsin
1982 (Gable), Iowa 130.25, Minnesota 49.75
  at Ann Arbor, Michigan
1983 (Gable), Iowa 200, Michigan State 81.5
  at Iowa City, Iowa
1984 (Gable), Iowa 175.75, Michigan State 103.25
  at East Lansing, Michigan
1985 (Gable), Iowa 195.5, Wisconsin 105.5
  at Evanston, Illinois
1986 (Gable), Iowa 169.75, Wisconsin 95
  at Minneapolis, Minnesota
1987 (Gable), Iowa 153, Wisconsin 121.5
  at Madison, Wisconsin

1988 (Gable), Iowa 116.75, Michigan 105.25
at Ann Arbor, Michigan

1989 (Gable), Iowa 125.25, Minnesota 113.75
at West Lafayette, Indiana

1990 (Gable), Iowa 138, Indiana 108.75
at Evanston, Illinois

1991 (Gable), Iowa 164, Michigan 92.5
at Champaign, Illinois

1992 (Gable), Iowa 185, Wisconsin 104
at Madison, Wisconsin

1993 (Gable), Iowa 128, Penn State 123.5
at Columbus, Ohio

1994 (Gable), Iowa 118, Minnesota 104.25
at Iowa City, Iowa

1995 (Gable), Iowa 185, Michigan State 109.5
at Bloomington, Indiana

1996 (Gable), Iowa 154.5, Penn State 92
at East Lansing, Michigan

1997 (Gable), Iowa 140.5, Minnesota 116.5
at Minneapolis, Minnesota

1998 (Zalesky), Iowa 132.5, Penn State 120.5
at State College, Pennsylvania

The Sun Rises, the Sun Sets

I didn't have many disputes with my parents growing up, but there was a time shortly after my sister died when my mom and I were struggling in our relationship. It was most likely stubbornness on my part, though I don't remember exactly what the issue was. I just remember that things weren't right between us.

Our dispute had gone on for quite a few days, when one night my dad and I were alone at home. We were sitting in the living room and he looked over at me and said, "Son, you just don't get it."

His words startled me.

He continued, "You don't get it at all. You have no idea what your mom thinks of you. You have no idea. Your mother would do anything for you. She thinks the sun rises on you and that the sun sets on you."

I will never forget my father saying that to me. It was so powerful that, whatever the issue was between my mom and me, it just instantly disappeared with no further thought. My only concern was my mom and how much I had been hurting her over the past several days.

Our family had gone through enough pain already with Diane's murder, so my dad's words really resonated with me. I didn't want to cause my mom any more pain.

That line my father used, "Your mother thinks the sun rises on you and that the sun sets on you," came back to me several years later.

I was at a speaking engagement at an I-Club in northwest Iowa, and an older farmer pulled me aside. You could tell he had been farming for some time, since his hands were cracked by a lifetime of hard work. When he shook my hand, he put his other hand over our clasped hands and smiled. Then he said, "Let me tell you how important you are to the state of Iowa and how I look at you and the Iowa wrestling program. As sure as the sun is going to rise tomorrow morning, and as sure as the sun is going to set tomorrow night, the University of Iowa wrestling program, come spring, will win the NCAA wrestling championships."

When this tough old farmer said those words, it brought me right back to my family's living room and my father saying basically the same thing when I was a teenager. Just like my father had told me how much I meant to my mother, this man was telling me how much the University of Iowa wrestling team meant for the people of Iowa.

I always knew the people of Iowa were proud of Hawkeye wrestling, but this farmer brought it out clearly and really made me realize our impact. We were putting the face of Iowa in front of the world, just as this farmer was helping to feed the world.

I will never forget that, and it inspired me and motivated me even more for the future. It made me want, more than ever, to do right by the people of Iowa, just like my dad's words so many years before made me want to do right by my mom.

The Final Season

Early one morning in December of 1996, I jumped out of bed, and as my feet hit the floor, I crashed to the ground. It was tough to move, and it wasn't letting up. It was like I had gotten hit with an explosive takedown and then the tight ride followed. (I'm only imagining what that is like though, since I am the one who hits the takedown and the tight ride!) I couldn't get up, so Kathy quickly helped me back into bed. Hoping the pain would go away, I lay there, waiting. But the pain just wasn't letting up.

Kathy got me in to see an orthopedic specialist at the University of Iowa Hospital that day. I called my assistants at the office to make sure they ran the show without me. I'd been to practice almost every day for twenty-five years straight. I knew the culture of discipline and hard work was there, and things could move along without me, but I still needed to implement the fine points of coaching on a daily basis.

It turned out that this was a serious injury, and not just something I could work through: my hip had fractured and needed to be replaced. We scheduled an early January hip replacement surgery. I quickly developed a great relationship with Dr. Larry Marsh, a surgeon at the University of Iowa Hospital and the current chair of the orthopedics department. It's very important to try to build this kind of relationship, if one can, with the person who is going to help decide your future.

This all meant that I was going to have a lot of downtime, so I had to learn how to coach from my bedside or on crutches. This gave me more time to think and analyze, which ended up being very productive, both for me and for the team. It gave me the chance to realize our greatest strengths, and lesser strengths, in a way I never had before. If I hadn't been injured, I would have just spent more time working the wrestlers on the mat, instead of figuring out and correcting the real issues.

I was listening to a dual meet on the radio in early January, and freshman Kasey Gilliss had just lost a match. Something about it didn't sound right through the radio announcing, so I began thinking about his wrestling. Kasey came to Iowa with a certain high-risk style of wrestling that used a lot of big moves. We were really focusing on basic technique with him, and as a result, we were encouraging him to wrestle in this more basic style that was still new to him and therefore wasn't as effective.

I made a few calls from my hospital bed, saying it was time to let Kasey wrestle the best way he knew how. We told Kasey, "Go back to your way of wrestling, and if they are there, you can hit those leg shots we've been teaching you." This seemed to work well for Kasey, and as he started hitting his own moves of headlocks, hip tosses, foot sweeps, lateral drops, front headlocks, and go-behinds, more leg attacks opened up for him. A varied attack like that is great. When your opponent knows you can attack from everywhere, it puts fear into them. Kasey did this by mixing what he was best at with what we taught him.

Our 177-pounder, Tony Ersland, was another puzzle that needed to be solved. He was a great kid, really nice. He was so nice that it was tough for us to go hard on him. I soon realized that he reminded me of another athlete a few years back, Travis Fiser. Travis was another really nice guy, but he didn't give great performances until I started treating him pretty rough. I realized that this was what Tony needed as well. Anyway, it couldn't hurt trying since being nice to him wasn't working, and Tony wanted it so bad. It was his senior year, and his first year as a regular, so it was both his first and last!

But I quickly found that I just couldn't do it, I couldn't be mean to this nice young man. One day an opening appeared. I was hobbling around and entered the locker room during practice, and there was Tony in the corner with his head in his hands, crying.

"Tony!" I said, surprised to see him like this during practice.

He sobbed, "Coach, I've been waiting for these days my whole life. They're here now, and I'm not performing up to my ability!"

This broke my heart, but instead of joining in and sobbing with him, I knew I needed to be stern. It could have been the drugs from my recent surgery, but this time I got tough with him. I knew he needed it. "Tony," I said to him, "it's time to man up. You think this is tough? Wait until you go out in life, get a job, get married, have kids—now that's tough. And if you can't handle this, where are you heading?" It was one of those moments that you don't forget. Tony turned the corner and started to improve shortly after.

Our heavyweight, Wes Hand, was another one of the youngsters on the team. He was very good, but he either didn't know it yet, or he did know it, but something was holding him back mentally. I saw some really great skills and talent in him a few times early on, but because I did see it, I wanted it every time. Show me something once, and I learned to expect greatness. So we had to build up his confidence in himself and his skills. Once Wes's mind was in sync with his wrestling talent, he could do just about anything technical in the sport.

Jessie Whitmer, our lightweight, was a fifth-year senior like Tony Ersland, and he had real potential, too. He hadn't been in our starting lineup regularly the previous few years, which was an obstacle for him. He had been competing quite often at tournaments where more athletes were allowed to enter beyond the ten starting weight classes, and he had done okay at several of them. But during this final year of regular competition, he wasn't finishing his matches strong.

He really liked his girlfriend, now wife, Meredith, and it apparently really inspired him when she painted her toenails bright red. So he started painting his toenails bright red, and as he put on his socks and wrestling shoes before matches, that extra adrenaline helped fire him up. I noticed this spark and started making sure that his toenails were freshly painted before his matches. They always were, but I kept a small bottle of red nail polish close by, just in case!

The other six wrestlers in our lineup were already credentialed All-Americans led by Lincoln McIlravy and Joe Williams, both also returning NCAA champions. We had another NCAA champion, Jeff McGinness, on the sidelines, redshirting that year so he could get bigger and stronger. It worked, and he won another NCAA title the following year at a higher weight class. Still, this team struggled a bit this season with a 21–13 loss to Oklahoma State at the National Duals in Lincoln, Nebraska.

McIlravy suffered a concussion early on and had to sit out part of the season. It was especially difficult for him because Lincoln had such a crazy way of wrestling. "It was frustrating because the success I had at Iowa had been the result of a tremendous amount of hard work," says McIlravy. "The confidence I had was that I was better prepared than the other guys. That year I didn't have the ability to work as hard as I had the year before. I had a series of concussions that year and had to miss a good portion of the year. I couldn't even really work out that year. Even getting your heart rate up can affect a concussion.

"I went into the Big Tens pretty ill prepared, and even the nationals, since there really isn't enough time to get ready for that type of competition. It was a frustrating year and a challenging year.

The results were fine in the end, but the performances weren't what they could have been if I was healthy."

We struggled at the Big Ten championships, winning only two weight classes with Mark Ironside at 134 pounds and Lincoln McIlravy at 150 pounds, as well as winning the team championship by a somewhat narrow margin. I thought we could get by at the Big Tens, so I started out sitting in the stands with my crutches. That didn't last long, and within an hour I bolted to the stage, somehow without my crutches! It was one of those moments where your body just reacts without any thoughts. I found my way to my wrestlers' corners, and stayed there for the rest of the tournament.

On the way back to Iowa City, I made plans for our last phase of training before the NCAAs. It was only eleven days away at the University of Northern Iowa. I had already made the decision to step down after this tournament, but I didn't like the thought of stepping down without one final championship. I told myself, "What will be, will be!" That's easy to say, but I was still anxious about our results. These young men needed a jolt to bring them up a notch to win this final battle of the season. We needed something to make the difference between finishing number two in the country and number one.

We traveled home from the Big Tens Sunday night and started our final round of practices Tuesday afternoon. Tuesday's practice was a good tough one, and after it ended, I went into the office to continue planning. After a short time in the office, I did my nightly walk through the locker room and wrestling room, picking up a few items left by the wrestlers: sweatshirts, headgear, and so on. Stuff that, when stolen, cost the athletes a ton. The costs were inflated to encourage them not to lose things, but they still got left out sometimes. Peggy Jenn, the Iowa equipment manager, was proud that her plan worked pretty well, because once the wrestlers were charged for a lost item, they usually didn't come back for seconds.

When I walked into the wrestling room that night, I saw Mark Ironside slumped on the mat against a big structural column. He was sitting in his soaked workout clothes in a pool of sweat, mostly asleep. "What the heck are you doing still here?" I asked.

"Coach, I'm exhausted. I haven't recovered from the Big Tens yet," he said in a low, worn voice.

"Okay, up and at 'em," I told him, helping haul him to his feet. "Make sure you sauna and get plenty of cold water before you leave, with your lack of cooldown."

I kept waking up all that night, thinking about Ironside's looks and comments. My thoughts went back to 1994 and my last-minute training with the US World team and how that backfired. I realized that I couldn't make the same mistake again.

The 1994 World team had plenty of credentialed athletes, but they didn't look good two weeks out from competition. They were coming off a disappointing finish in the Goodwill Games, and upon watching them for the first two days of my arrival at training camp at Foxcatcher Farm, I didn't see any positives. As a result, I worked them too hard for too long and too far out of their routine habits too close to competition. It was too many toos.

I should have seen the positives in who they were and what they had already accomplished. My thinking normally is "Do it once and I expect it all the time." Instead, I only focused on all the negatives. We did win a couple of medals: Melvin Douglas took third at 198 pounds and Bruce Baumgartner took second at 286 pounds. But these days I wonder, how did we get those medals after what I put them through? With more time and better relationships between the athletes and the coaches, me included, that team could have won it all. It's better to go with what you have than to force-feed them. I force-fed them and they swallowed.

I had been involved with, but was not the actual head coach of, World or Olympic teams for ten years. I think this made the transition even tougher for both athletes and me as the coach. I would have been better off sliding in easy and not pushing the envelope. Then, we could have gone from there in the direction needed for more success.

This 1997 Hawkeye team was too close to the NCAA finals for me to really push them. They didn't look good, but they had been proven before. We had six All-Americans, two of whom held a total of three NCAA titles. I knew they could wrestle and wrestle well; I just had to make sure they felt good and were motivated.

At our 6:30 A.M. practice the next morning, we warmed up really well. Then, when they thought the wrestling was going to begin, I told them to hit the sauna and showers instead. They were so surprised they actually stood there and looked at me like I was kidding. Once they realized I was serious, they did so.

The rest of the time before the NCAAs was focused on good warm-ups and short blasts of wrestling. I stressed recovery, along with scoring, feeling good, and team bonding. To this day, I thank God I ran into Ironside that night! He was the heartbeat of the team, and his own heart was pounding from exhaustion.

So the stage was set.

Kasey Gilliss started the Hawks off with a planned two-on-one tie, which led to a foot sweep to a headlock to a pin. The Hawks won a record number of matches in a row on the second day, and that disrupted the trophy presenters. The tournament administrators apparently expected the Hawkeyes to come in second, because my high school coach, Bob Siddens, was set to present the award to the runner-up team. After our sweep of victories that day though, I heard his name called over the sound system: "Bob Siddens, come to the head table." They changed his role so he was now presenting the award to the championship team.

We had six wrestlers in the finals after day two, with two others still going for third place. Two wrestlers lost their pivotal match in their quest to become All-Americans in the last round on Friday night.

On the final day, Mike Uker ended up taking fifth, and Kasey Gilliss ended up sixth, both All-Americans. This was Uker's second time as an All-American.

During the finals, five out of six of our wrestlers won. Mike Mena was the only defeat that day, and that was in overtime. I actually made a mistake with Mena in our team meeting after the semis that Friday night. Mena was a senior and a four-time All-American who hadn't made it to the finals before. In that meeting, I noticed he was enjoying his semis win and still had a smile on his face. I saw it but decided to let him enjoy it, thinking he would refocus shortly. This was a mistake. The next day after the wrestlebacks, we had another meeting, and Mena had the same smirk. He should have had the proper game face on before he went to sleep. I quickly told him that it was time to focus on what's next: the finals. I hoped it was enough time, for he still had all afternoon. Obviously it wasn't enough though. It's not that he wrestled poorly, just not as well as he needed to. The lesson here is, move your focus on to the next thing, not what you've already done.

Still, it was an outstanding performance for the Hawkeyes, as Lee Fullhart ended the evening with an escape in overtime to win our last match, and it set a record that still holds. Everyone who wrestled contributed vital individual points to that record-setting team performance:

1st place: Iowa—170 points (record performance)
2nd place: Oklahoma State—113.5 points
118—Jessie Whitmer, 1st place
126—Mike Mena, 2nd place
134—Mark Ironside, 1st place
142—Kasey Gilliss, 6th place

150—Lincoln McIlravy, 1st place

158—Joe Williams, 1st place

167—Mike Uker, 5th place

177—Tony Ersland, lost in the final round to the number one
seed in the tournament to place

190—Lee Fullhart, 1st place

HWT—Wes Hand, lost in the final round to place

"There were a lot of exciting things going on that year," says Mc-Ilravy of it now. "It was my senior year, and it was the last year Coach Gable ever coached. The nationals were at UNI, so there were a lot of Hawkeye fans there, and then to set the point record like that. I don't think anybody thought we had that ability going in, and I don't think anyone was worried about it. But we were very well prepared, and even Gable did some of his best coaching that year.

"One of the things that's so impressive with Coach Gable over the years is that the situations are always different and your athletes are different, and he found ways to adapt to all those variables, including his health at the time, and be very, very successful."

Crazy but True

In all my time wrestling and coaching wrestling, there have been a lot of times that created crazy stories. These are just a few.

THE LEAP AND THE CHEEK PINCH

Dan Wagemann was a little different, a goofy kid who wound up finishing second in the NCAA championships in 1976.

One time, when I was an assistant coach at Iowa, we were at Iowa State wrestling before a loud, packed house. Dan and his opponent were wrestling near the edge of the mat. Dan's opponent backed up to the center to get away from the edge, and Wagemann ran at the guy from the edge of the mat. Wagemann took his momentum and jumped up over his opponent's head in a move that people now call "The Squirrel." When Wagemann went over the guy's head, he was able to grab the back of his opponent's legs and upper hip, while his opponent grabbed Wagemann's knees. This led to an incredible scramble that had the crowd on its feet. Wagemann eventually controlled the hips and ended up getting the takedown to win the match in front of fourteen thousand wrestling fans, the majority of whom were cheering for Iowa State.

They certainly weren't happy!

At another Iowa State meet, Wagemann was wrestling a tough match, and the official made a call Dan didn't agree with. Rather than letting me discuss it with the official, Wagemann went up to the official, reached up, and pinched and shook his cheek. The crowd went wild, and through all the noise of the people in the stands, the official disqualified Wagemann, threw him out of the match, and awarded six team points to the other team.

"I could ride anybody in the country with my legs," remembers Wagemann. "They called me Crazy Legs Wags, or some people even called me an octopus. He kept getting up, and I'd throw a leg in on him, and the referee, Keith Young, didn't like what he was seeing. He considered it a stall move. So he gave me a stall warning and a point to the other guy. Then he called one more stalling point after that, so I just walked up to him and gently tweaked his cheek with a pinch.

"The referee said, 'You're out of here.' The meet was against Iowa State, so I gave the maximum amount of points away to the other team. My teammates weren't angry with me, but they were trying to get me off the mat and away from things.

"Would I do it again? Probably."

When he came off the mat, I didn't say much to Wagemann at the moment, because now the next match was even more crucial. But did it surprise me? Yes, it did. That was my first and last cheek tweak. But really, I had to consider the source: Wagemann was a little goofy. After that, both Wagemann and I had to be more prepared for the unknown and the surprising. I gave him some extra mentoring to help us both in the future, too.

NO LOVE LOST

Michigan was probably our biggest rival in the Big Ten back in 1974. We were getting pretty good crowds, two or three thousand people in the old Field House at this point, but we were always looking for ways to increase those numbers.

At our weekly press conference just before a big home meet with

Michigan, head coach Gary Kurdelmeier made his thoughts known: "We don't like Michigan, and they don't like us." The next day, that quote was on the front page of the local newspaper. As you would expect, that generated a lot of excitement in Iowa City and throughout the state. Those were fighting words!

The crowd turned out to be much bigger than normal, and they were certainly ready for some action. We lost as a team, but it was a close loss, and there was definitely action.

On the swing match, Dan Holm was winning when, accidentally or not, his opponent gave him an extra jolt and he reacted by swearing. The official immediately disqualified him. That was the difference that caused us to lose as a team, but in some ways, it helped. There were so many fans there, and they went wild. After that, they came back.

"I was wrestling at 167 pounds," Holm remembers. "I got taken down in the first period, and he put a figure-four cross-body ride on me. The first period ended, the referee blew the whistle, and he turned around and walked back to the center of the mat. While his back was turned, Michigan gave me an extra pop with the figure four. So I rolled on my side, threw an elbow, and called him an SOB. That's what the referee heard, but he didn't see it.

"So I got disqualified. I kept my temper. I didn't say anything else. I was the type of guy to take it to the limit, but not break the rules. The next night, we wrestled Michigan State and I put a pounding on that guy, 17–0. I tried to pin him, but I couldn't, so I put a whooping on him instead."

Even though we lost to Michigan that night, it got people talking and excited about following Iowa wrestling for the future. In the long run, that benefited the team and the sport more than the results of one night of wrestling would have.

KNITTING

When I first got to Iowa as an assistant coach, I was looking to win right away. I saw the raw talent we had in our wrestling room, and I believed that if I could apply the kind of training I received at West Waterloo, Iowa State, and during my Olympic training to this group, we could be very successful right away.

Kurdelmeier, on the other hand, was looking to win of course, but he was focused on building the team long-term. He said we had a five-year building process and saw the really serious winning as something we were building toward.

He was being more realistic than I was, and of course, he had been coaching much longer. What I didn't know yet was that even though some of these guys had the physical talent, their minds weren't developed yet. I didn't understand the importance of mental toughness at first, whereas Kurdelmeier did. I had always been around mental toughness, so I didn't know that not everyone comes into that level of wrestling with it already in place.

We met somewhere in the middle, because we won the national championship in three years, during the 1974–75 season. So I learned a lesson not to overestimate, and Kurdelmeier learned a lesson not to underestimate. Yet we were on an upward swing all throughout those three years.

At the beginning, the younger guys were working with me on my type of training right from the start, but the older guys had to be eased into it, because it was more intense than what they were used to. One of the older guys was Jan Sanderson. He worked really hard during practice, but when practice was over, it was over. He wasn't one to stay after. We had several guys like that, and I knew to let them be the way they were. I didn't like that approach to training, but I understood it and accepted that not everyone trained the same way I did.

Jan still ended up being a two-time All-American, placing sixth at the 1972 NCAA tournament at 158 pounds and third at 167 pounds in 1974. He wasn't on that first national championship team, but he was on the rise and was a talented guy. He also taught me a valuable lesson about letting wrestlers be themselves.

Jan wrestled toward the end of the meet, and was usually about the seventh guy out of ten weight classes. My philosophy for the guys was that, if they weren't wrestling for a while, they probably shouldn't be out watching unless they knew how to relax and not waste energy. Jan knew how to relax: he knitted. He would sit there on the bench before his match, knitting scarves, socks, hats, and sweaters.

"Knitting was unusual, I guess, but nobody seemed to mind," Sanderson says about it now. "I got a lot of press for it. You sit around and wait. A lot of times, it's stressful and tense. It was a relaxing activity. I gave everything away. I mainly just made scarves and stocking hats. They were easy to give away.

"It might have been a psychological advantage in some cases. When I wrestled in high school, I had cloth headgear, a real old one that looked like old boxing headgear. I would soak that in rose water, which is like cheap perfume. People would tie up with me, and they'd smell that, and it would give them a little pause, and it would slow them up for a few seconds at the beginning. I don't know what they were thinking, but I know they weren't thinking about wrestling. They were thinking about something other than wrestling, so it had to be some kind of an advantage."

Jan's knitting was certainly unusual, but it kept his mind off the match, so he didn't waste energy. He was successful on the mat, at least in part because he knew how to keep his mind where he wanted it to be. Knitting worked for him, and that lesson helped me with my own transition into coaching.

STAR-STRUCK

On December 21, 2013, Penn State came to Iowa City for a dual against the Iowa Hawkeyes. Two A-list actors, Ashton Kutcher and his then-fiancée Mila Kunis, sat next to me at the meet. Kutcher was born in Cedar Rapids, Iowa, and wrestled when he was younger and attended Clear Creek Amana High School in Iowa. He is an avid Iowa Hawkeye fan and a good wrestling fan.

Since we were in the first row, hundreds of people came down the stairs to get their autographs in between bouts. Ashton and Mila left their seats at one point, and I noticed there was a teenage girl pacing back and forth on the arena floor. I flagged her down and told her that Ashton and Mila would be right back.

Her response? "I've been waiting to get your autograph, not theirs." I certainly wasn't expecting that.

WRESTLING WITH HOLLYWOOD

In April 1973, an article about my life entitled "Gorgeous Dan" ran in *Esquire* magazine. I was still fresh off my win at the 1972 Olympics and was deeply entrenched in my new profession as an assistant wrestling coach at the University of Iowa when the article ran. The author, John Irving, was a former wrestler and wrestling coach, and was teaching creative writing at the University of Iowa Writers' Workshop at the time. John stopped by the wrestling room from time to time for workouts with the team. He is a lifelong wrestling fan and one of our sport's greatest advocates.

Irving has become one of the most recognized figures in wrestling and in writing. He has written numerous books, five of which have been made into films. In 2000, he won an Academy Award for Best Adapted Screenplay for *The Cider House Rules*. That night was the only time I ever stayed up to watch the Academy Awards.

John has never forgotten his time in Iowa City and working out with the Hawkeyes and me. I'm still surprised by how much I inspired him though:

"It's one thing to be an example of excellence as an athlete. It's quite another to have an effect on people where, psychologically—and in their hearts—you make them want to be better than they are," John writes today.

"This was a time in my life where I felt sorry for myself. I wasn't well-enough known as a writer in my estimation. I didn't have enough time to write in my estimation. I loved my kids, but my marriage wasn't going so well.

"We were driving somewhere one night, and Dan said something to me along the lines of, 'Things aren't going too well for you right now, are they?' He recognized that things weren't perfect with me. And he said something along the lines of, 'You can do something about that, you know.' He pretty much said that if something is wrong, you can fix it, and you're the only one. It was rather matter-of-fact. It was a small moment.

"Writers, by reputation, have disastrous lives. Everybody did. Nobody is going to tell you that you can do anything about it. I wasn't a kid. I was older than he was. I remember thinking, 'The next time I see you, pal, I'm going to be doing better than I am.'

"The night I won an Oscar for *Cider House Rules,* I was out in Beverly Hills, and I got back to the hotel at five in the morning or something. There were a number of my writer friends who certainly knew I was there, and some of them probably knew where I was staying. And I didn't hear from anybody. I was probably out on the West Coast for not quite a week before I came back to Vermont. I looked through the messages on my answering machine and there wasn't a single message from any of my writer friends saying congratulations—but there was a message from Gable.

"Gable put it in an interesting way. I used to say to him, when we would talk about wrestling or something, that I never won a tournament at any level of the sport. And the message on my machine was, 'Hey, you finally won something.' It made me feel good that he was thinking about it. He wrote me later that it was way past his bedtime, and it was the only time he stayed up for the Academy Awards."

SAY WHAT?

People have attributed a lot of quotes to me over the course of my career. Some I actually said, some I question. This is my chance to set the record straight:

"Once you have wrestled, everything else in life is easy."

That is definitely my quote, though my 1972 Olympic coach, Bill Farrell, who has since passed away, claimed I stole it from him. He may have said something like that earlier in his career, but if he did, I never heard it and never saw it published. So as far as I'm concerned, that's my quote.

"Wrestling isn't for everyone—but it should be."

That is definitely, 100 percent something I said. There is something that everyone can get out of the sport of wrestling, and everyone can learn some great life skills from it. I'm pretty proud of that quote.

"Gold medals really aren't made out of gold. They are made of sweat, determination, and a hard-to-find alloy called guts."

I've been given credit for saying this because somebody who interviewed me published it. I didn't say that exactly, but he put my words together the way he wanted and came out with that quote. I have no problem with it, but it wasn't exactly the way I said it.

"More enduringly than any other sport, wrestling teaches self-control and pride. Some have wrestled without great skill. None have wrestled without pride."

That's me again, but it's from another writer who took several things I said during an interview, put them together, and created a quote. I probably said all of those things, but not in that way.

"The first period is won by the best technician. The second period is won by the kid in the best shape. The third period is won by the kid with the biggest heart."

I don't think I said that, as it's not really my philosophy.

"I shoot, I score. He shoots, I score."

That's mine all the way. Totally.

"My valleys are higher than most people's peaks."

I absolutely said that. I'm the guy who always planned things out in advance. I drew charts, so I had a system of peaking. That's definitely me.

"Bad habits are like a good bed: easy to get into, but difficult to get out of."

I'm not sure where this quote came from. When you're really motivated and really focused, it is really easy to get out of bed. I've seen that when Ed Banach worked out at 4:30 in the morning. I proved that during all the years we had practice at six in the morning toward the end of the season. When you're not motivated or you don't have something to focus on, you want to stay in bed when you wake up. I measure my motivation by whether I want to lie there, or if I want to get up. When I want to lie there, I know I need to get more focused. If it's difficult to get up day after day, then you need to refocus and find something meaningful in your life to make you want to get your butt out of bed.

A MESSY SITUATION

Current University of Iowa head wrestling coach Tom Brands says that when you wrestle, you either go out there and give it all you have, or you poop your pants. He tells his team that so they give an all-out effort. He doesn't want them to be scared, he doesn't want them to be shy, and he doesn't want them to not live up to their potential.

I'll tell you how tough I am: I can do both. In my freshman year, at my first major tournament, the 1966 Midlands, I went out during the first round, went gangbusters, and won the match—but I also pooped my pants. I was using some extra effort and my gas tank was on full. I won the tournament.

RETRIBUTION

They say it's tougher to win on the road, but wrestling against Oklahoma State is never easy, home or away. The Cowboys were still the top-ranked team in the country when Iowa State wrestled Oklahoma State in Stillwater on February 9, 1968. It was my sophomore season at Iowa State, and this was my first time wrestling in Stillwater as a college competitor. We had lost 15–14 to Oklahoma State at home the month before, so this was our chance to get even with the Cowboys. Instead, the referee got even with us.

I was the third wrestler up when I faced off against Ray Murphy at 137 pounds. Ray was a good wrestler who became an All-American later that year and an NCAA tournament runner-up the following year. I wrestled hard and won 6–5, but when the match was over, instead of raising my hand, the referee raised both our hands. He said the score was 6–6. The coaches got in an argument, and, finally, after a long discussion, the referee came back out and only raised my hand. I got a one-point win, though I don't recall any of his five points actually being scored.

Points kept being given in favor of Oklahoma State throughout the entire dual. We lost 23–5, and I was the only wrestler to win that night. Jason Smith of Iowa State and Bob Drebenstedt of Oklahoma State tied at 167 pounds.

The crowd that night apologized to us as they were leaving, and the city of Stillwater, Oklahoma, actually sent an apology that was published in the *Des Moines Register*, saying that the officiating was not appropriate and that the referee made many bad calls. Years later, I became pretty good friends with Oklahoma State head wrestling coach Myron Roderick, and he told me that the referee owed him some money at the time, and he thinks the guy was trying to pay him off with wrestling points, so he would take some of that debt away.

In 1993 when I was the head wrestling coach at Iowa, we won a tough dual against Minnesota at home, 21–13. Minnesota head wrestling coach J Robinson, who used to be on my coaching staff at Iowa, was upset about the referee's calls in one of the matches. As we were walking out of the arena, he said to me, "I'm going to get you, Gable. I'm going to get you."

The next year, we wrestled Minnesota in Minneapolis. I didn't think we were going to get another referee like the one in Stillwater in 1968, but it was the second-worst referee I ever saw in terms of intentional calls against the visiting team. It happened from the beginning of the meet until the end, and Iowa lost 23–11. It wasn't like the meet in Stillwater, but the calls were still more one-sided than I felt they should have been.

I was upset at first, but after the third match, I realized that these calls were not making the difference between who was winning and losing. We could have won the meet, even with this referee, if our guys would have stepped up to the occasion. Instead of making their own breaks though, they gave the referee an opportunity to make some terrible calls. I used the meet as a learning tool for our guys though, and it got our team more ready for the big battles coming up at the end of the season.

Sometimes, an unfair environment can make all the difference when it really counts.

TAKING THE PRESSURE OFF

It was the 1990–91 season, and the Iowa Hawkeyes were feeling the pressure of defending seventeen straight Big Ten titles, yet they also still needed to grow more in order to start another string of NCAA championships. We had a solid lineup that year: Chad Zaputil (118), Terry Brands (126), Tom Brands (134), Troy Steiner (142), Terry Steiner (150), Tom Ryan (158), Mark Reiland (167), Bart Chelesvig (177), Travis Fiser (190), and John Oostendorp (HWT).

We had continued an unbroken streak of Big Ten titles but had ended our NCAA title streak in 1987 after nine straight victories. We had not won an NCAA team title since then, but this team definitely had the potential. Still, we were feeling the pressure of our own history.

Years earlier, at the 1979 Big Ten tournament, I decided to sit in the stands for the finals. I felt that the pressure of our winning streak of five straight conference titles was getting to our team. We needed to win almost every match in the last session to beat Wisconsin for this title; plus, the Big Tens were in Iowa City this year, so we had an even greater need to win at home. I knew I needed to take pressure off the team, so I told them I was going to sit in the stands and enjoy the evening, eating popcorn and yelling. We won.

This is where we were again in 1991. After a National Duals loss to Penn State, a team that we had defeated earlier in the season by twenty-six points, I knew I needed to back off again. The next important dual was at Iowa State University: another high-pressure event, given our in-state rivalry. I told our team how great their potential was, but, "By being in your corner in potentially tough situations, I'm causing you to hold back. I know you guys want to win so badly, especially for me and everyone associated with the program, but how about wanting to win for you?"

So on January 20, 1991, I went up into the stands and took a seat. There were a number of open seats directly above where the Iowa team was sitting on the floor, which I thought was odd, but I took a seat there anyway. It turned out that these empty seats were reserved for the Iowa State pep band. The Hawkeye wrestling team thought it was hilarious when band members dressed in cardinal and gold, with musical instruments, surrounded me. The Iowa team kept them quiet most of the night though, and we won, 25–9. When Iowa State did win a match, my ears rang from the pep band's loud music all around me.

This 1991 team not only brought the Iowa glory back home to Iowa City that night, but they also won the Big Tens by 71.5 points later that year, and the NCAA title by 48.25 points, over second-place Oklahoma State. We were back in the national champion seat.

In both cases, in 1979 and in 1991, I really was holding the team back. I was putting too much pressure on those kids. They were freezing up, so I decided to remove myself from the mat corner and take the pressure off. It worked!

CELEBRATIONS OF OLD

The Hawkeyes won their first NCAA title in wrestling in 1975. This was big news since it was only the second NCAA team title in school history (the gymnastics team won Iowa's first-ever NCAA title in 1969). NCAA titles never come easy, though some outsiders may have thought so during Iowa's run of wrestling titles, which currently stands at twenty-three and counting.

That first 1975 title led to quite a few crazy celebrations. The most memorable of those celebrations occurred when a farmer southwest of Iowa City hosted a party on his grassy fields, complete with 110 sixteen-gallon kegs. The whole school was invited, and thousands of students and community members came to party and celebrate the Hawks' victory.

I thought the kicker came when a plane flew over the party site with a banner congratulating the team. But then, they kicked it up another notch, and people started parachuting out of the plane. Those of us on the ground quickly realized that the skydivers, both male and female, were naked from the waist down below their long shirts. They made quite an entrance and, wow, what a cheering section they had when they landed!

Of course, this sort of thing could not happen today; if it did, there would be unpleasant consequences for all involved. But wow, what a party!

THE CALL

In 1992, Bobby Douglas was hired as the new head wrestling coach at Iowa State after an eighteen-year stint at Arizona State, which included an NCAA team championship in 1988. On his first day on the job as the Cyclone head wrestling coach, he decided to call my house at six in the morning to let me know that he was on the job and that he was going to outwork me. My wife, Kathy, answered the phone and let him know that I had already gone to work, catching a plane to recruit an athlete to Iowa. Bobby didn't say much after that, hoping Kathy was kidding. No kidding here!

Regrets—Not Many

When I was in my individual competitive days as an athlete, I was sometimes referred to as the guy who never smiled. I never believed that was totally true; it was just that most people saw me when I had my game face on. Of course, that was most of the time, so I can understand their thinking. It was a rare moment when I was distracted enough to smile around other wrestlers, though I know it did happen occasionally.

As time passed and I grew into my coaching profession, I must have allowed myself to smile and laugh more around others. With all the winning and celebrating we were doing, it was bound to have shone through.

So it shocked me when, not too long ago, during a conversation with my wife, she looked me directly in the eyes and said, "It wasn't until you stopped being the coach that you ever smiled or joked around."

"What? Come on, that can't be true, and I don't believe it," I told her.

She simply responded, "Ask your daughters."

So that is what I did, and I was surprised at how much they backed her up.

This made me think hard, and I actually went back over my day-to-day routine over the years to figure out where this was coming from. I was good at this sort of personal reflection, since I had done it before after various major setbacks.

After doing a lot of searching and reflection, this was my explanation:

In the early and mid-1980s, there were times that I should have headed straight home after a full day, but instead, I often made a quick stop to unwind, making long days even longer. Sometimes I swung by a bar or a friend's house; other times, I drove the country roads, talking to a coach or athlete. Sometimes I went out into the country by myself, looking for wildlife, such as pheasants or deer, and thinking. With Kathy, Jenni, Annie, and Molly at home (Mackie arrived in 1988), I should have been spending that time with them instead. My priority should have been taking care of business, both at work and at home, and not necessarily in that order. Of all the times in my life, this period is one of the hardest and most difficult for me to accept, yet also the most necessary to prevent repeating in the future.

At that time, I generally dropped the girls off at school in the morning, unless we had an early morning practice. I usually got home around 7:00 P.M. and had a late dinner with the girls, unless I got home later than that; then, I only got to tuck them into bed. When you are coming home from a fifty-person wrestling practice, where at least half of that group would be somewhat upset, the coach might not be in the best of moods. Under those circumstances, I can see myself not smiling or joking around much. So, yes, I suppose the limited amount of time I got to spend with my family, and the mood I was in when I did, probably did impact the way they saw me in those days.

So, looking back to December of 1996, when I jumped out of bed for one of those early morning practices, and crashed to the floor instead with a fractured hip, I have to ask myself, was it really this injury that got me out of coaching at age forty-eight? No, I just needed some reconstructive surgery, and I could handle that. It was really the mental stress and strain that I had been under for some time that needed to change. This stress tended to drain away during the season for a short time as we racked up wins. Then it would start coming back in the last month or so of each season, and be gone again at the end of the season. Of course, if we ended in second place, it never really went away.

I always say that if I had stayed in coaching much longer, I would not be here writing this second book, let alone have written my first book. My life on earth would have been over years ago.

Now I am able to focus on my family and wrestling, *in that order*. Also, my focus in wrestling these days is more on promotion and product quality. I do all kinds of speaking on performance, excellence, and adversity, hopefully in an entertaining fashion. Some people have even called me the funniest person they know. I don't know about that, but maybe I have more than one game face now. Plus, I'm still alive.

So I do have a few regrets, and I do owe a few apologies.

To my wife, kids, and many others: I want you to know that I had a lot of internal smiling and happiness, even if you couldn't see it from the outside.

Cartered, Bushed, Trumped, and the IOC

Because of the high goals and accomplishments closely associated with my life, there have been several incidents of interest or controversy worth mentioning.

As an athlete during the early seventies, especially in battles against tough USSR wrestlers, there were references often to the Cold War going on and winning that war. At the time, I really did not understand the rhetoric, but it seemed to add fuel to my competitive fires. Anyway, the positive results showed it was working!

It continued on with my coaching of international teams, especially with USA national teams versus the USSR teams. Winning as an athlete is one thing that can be done effectively, but winning as a team then was more difficult because of the dominance of the USSR in wrestling. But anything is possible, and, yes, this is what you dream about and do if you're an idealistic thinker. That's me, so, yes, we (the USA wrestlers) with me as the 1980 Olympic freestyle team coach were heading to the 1980 Moscow Olympics to defeat the USSR team in their home country.

Of course it didn't happen. No, we weren't defeated, we didn't go to the 1980 Moscow Olympics in protest of the Soviet invasion of Afghanistan. Other countries followed suit, making for a less than total Olympic Games. President Jimmy Carter pulled the plug for the USA to participate. The president makes the call, and you back the call. Why? Out of respect for the highest position of authority for your country. Was it the right call? Many debates and other after-the-fact calls can be discussed and conclusions drawn. To each their own. That's America! No defeat of the USSR wrestling team is what I know.

■ ■ ■

The sport of amateur wrestling, especially at the collegiate level, was taking a hit during the late 1990s and early 2000s. Wrestling's leaders and strategies weren't the best in helping during this time. I had stepped down from coaching the University of Iowa wrestling team and now had more time to recover my health and focus on areas of legislative needs for wrestling and other Olympic sports. The President's Council on Physical Fitness actually appointed me to their group.

President George Bush was at the helm, and I was to meet him at the Des Moines airport as the greeter for one of his visits to Iowa. I figured I could use some of his advice on the issues of college sports and Olympic sports for the future. So, yes, besides being his greeter, I figured I could get and give some information to him in this area for the future. As he deplaned and reached out to shake my already forward hand, he whispered in my ear, "Can you believe Iowa State University dropped baseball?" I thought for a second on his lead words and knew I didn't need any further discussion with President Bush about this, for he was already on top of it. Enough said, he's the president of the United States.

■ ■ ■

I did not initially know Donald Trump's background or that his campaign team would be reaching out to me. When I was doing a book signing in Cherokee, Iowa, for *A Wrestling Life*, a Trump staff advisor conversed with me about supporting him. This advisor, Chris Hupke, gave me his business card. That was the start to an interesting ride that was informing and intriguing even to date. I already knew that Trump was part of a wrestling team during his high school days, but later learned his son Donald Jr. had wrestled for several years while growing up. So, yes, he had that in common with me, and this instigated several face-to-face meetings with him and members of his family and another Trump advisor, Tana Goertz.

Of course, having Iowa Governor Terry Branstad backing Trump helped big time, and the fact that Donald Trump worked Iowa heavily pushed him to victory in Iowa and to the presidency. Yes, Secretary of State Hillary Clinton worked nonstop as well, but my contacts were all one-sided and have been so since Bush.

The slogans of "Make America great again" (Trump) or "Stronger together" (Clinton) are really only determined once they step down and look back at them and then what they are doing currently, so, yes, it's a never-ending process and evaluation.

For me, I had a very good home life when I was a kid. With good directions, it led to another very good high school and college career athletically. The academic end was good, but maybe not as good as the athletic credentials. Then the coaching career was very good, along with the family career, measuring up quite similarly. Nothing is perfect, yet you can come close, so I'm still working for that greatness that I pursue in my future. It will come down to my faith and continued determination. For America, the slogans of both Trump and Clinton are the answer. In a divided democracy and government, the answer is best summed up by saying, "Make America great again by being stronger together." This is something that appears difficult, but many great performances in all of life have happened. And most if not all happened with teamwork! It can happen, but appears easier said than done in government. Time will tell!

■ ■ ■

In 2013, the International Olympic Committee voted wrestling out of the Olympics after 2016. Wrestling's governing body, FILA, had to perform miracle work to get it back in. What FILA did was change leadership at the top and emphasize all the people, not just part of the population.

International wrestling's governing body is now called United World Wrestling (UWW). They replaced their leader, and Nenad Lalovic of Serbia took on the new role of president. Immediately, he started working to get one of the spots on the IOC, something that was lacking with wrestling. Why? Because of the poor thinking that wrestling was untouchable since it was one of the original Olympic sports, wrestling felt a sense of entitlement. Sorry, but one needs to contribute. No one is entitled, and when you think you are, you won't be for long.

Good leadership and ongoing contributions to the cause or causes important to you are the best ways to stay ahead in your game or relationship, working together in great ways. Sounds familiar, and yes, it worked for wrestling, but it must continue. Our representative on the old FILA board is Stan Dziedzic, former World wrestling champion (1977) and current vice president of UWW. Stan led the comeback along with a USA Wrestling committee named the Committee for the Preservation of Olympic Wrestling (CPOW). Rich Bender (executive director for USA Wrestling), Bill Scherr (World champion, 1985), and several others were members, myself included. I called this committee Ka-POW, for it had an effective way of getting things done. The resources brought in were phenomenal and allowed for quick action that led to accomplishments. Thanks here to several people who had these resources to give and did! The rest of the wrestling world pitched in as well with resources, politics, and events that brought a lot of good attention and information to the sport of wrestling.

Working together and winning together put wrestling back into prominence, yet a culture takes time to really change. Again, time will tell!

The Run for or From

In early 2001, Iowa Republican leader Chuck Larson Jr. called me up to discuss whether I had any interest in running for governor of Iowa. Our conversation went a little over my head in some ways, and running for political office was not part of my plans at that point. Still, I agreed to talk to state Republican party officials a bit more and see if maybe this was something that I wanted to pursue.

This exploratory process was somewhat overwhelming, and I had extensive meetings over the next four months. One of the first conversations I had with state party leadership was the result of a simple question that I answered at least partially incorrectly. The question was very simple: "Are you a Republican?"

My answer was, "I might be. Or maybe an independent?"

When voting, I only took an interest in the person, not the party. Party officials looked into my status and found out that I had been a registered Democrat for twenty-five years, which certainly surprised me. So I had to officially change over and become a registered Republican.

After that, for the next four months, I had personal, one-on-one meetings that were quite extensive. I met with people like former Iowa Speaker of the House Ron Corbett and attorney Doug Gross. I really enjoyed those meetings, and everyone treated me very well. I was getting some pressure to make a decision though, as time was running out before I would have to launch an official campaign, if I did decide to run.

During this process, I realized that there is one major element in politics that is very different from my experiences coaching for the NCAA and the USA Olympic teams. That element is that there are no rules in government. Nothing is prohibited: all is fair in government and war, apparently.

Also, one reporter portrayed me in a very negative light in an interview he conducted with me. When published, he made structural changes without my permission. Now that's power: untrue power. But it was done. I could refute what he said, but he had the pen and the final say, so I decided to let it lie. There was enough good out there in my life that I did not want to let this bring me down to his level.

Not long before decision time, I had a final personal meeting in Des Moines with Branstad. On my way to Des Moines, I went through Marshalltown for some reason. It was lunchtime as I was passing through, and I'm a fan of Maid-Rite, an Iowa chain that serves loose-meat sandwiches, and I knew that the original Maid-Rite was located here. As I walked into the historic Marshalltown Taylor's Maid-Rite for lunch, I saw that only one seat was available at the square bar.

The *Des Moines Register* had just announced my possible run for governor that day, and it was front-page news. Sitting down at the bar, I saw that a *Register* was face up on the counter with the Gable name plastered along the top. Fortunately, no one looked up, as they were all busy enjoying their sandwiches. I was glad, since I was not ready for any political conversations just yet.

The waitress walked over, and I ordered a Cheese-Rite. Every face around that square-top bar looked up with a gasp and stared at me. I didn't realize the error I'd just made, and the waitress immediately said, "Sir, no cheese."

For those who don't know, it's taboo to order anything but a Maid-Rite with onion, pickle, and mustard at the Taylor's Maid-Rite in Marshalltown. Not totally understanding my mistake yet, I decided to go with what was safe and responded, "I'll have a Maid-Rite!"

"Fine," she said, and all heads went back down to their sandwiches.

My next statement was another disaster though: "Can I get some ketchup with that Maid-Rite?" All the faces looked back up at me, and there was another gasp. I had made another major misstep and recovered with, "Just a Maid-Rite, please?" Though I will say that now, after eighty-six years, Taylor's Maid-Rite in Marshalltown does have ketchup available on all the tables, so maybe I really did know what I was talking about then.

Anyway, no one in there said anything to me about a run for governor. If I couldn't handle ordering a Maid-Rite correctly, running for governor was out of the question. I ate my sandwich quietly, and then quickly left for my meeting.

I had met with Governor Branstad before, but this meeting was tougher. This time, Branstad had his game face on. We talked privately for a short time, and then he brought in Marvin Pomerantz, a prominent Des Moines businessman and political advisor. I got kind of confused at this point, as both guys now had that same game face on. I felt outnumbered. In reality, I had already been outnumbered during my private meeting with just Branstad.

I was still bouncing back and forth on whether or not to run, and they knew it, so they took the step of setting up some meetings for me with party leadership in Washington, DC. This time though, I took some backup with me: my former wrestler and now friend, Mitch Kelly. Mitch has always been interested in politics, and I knew he could steer me straight, or at least help out if needed.

The day in DC went well. I met with several other state governors, and I was actually leaning toward running. Maybe. Toward the end of the day, I had one last meeting with a top Bush advisor, Karl Rove. I really wasn't that familiar with him, but I figured they were saving the best for last.

The meeting was mostly one-sided: his side, as it should be. After all, he's the expert on politics, not me.

The conversation was short. "Coach, you're done being the coach."

"Yes, I know, I've been done for a few years," I responded.

"No, I mean you are done thinking," he said. "You do what we tell you now."

I came back with, "I need to use some of my own judgment. It's worked pretty well so far, both on and off the mat."

With that, the conversation was pretty much over, and we departed.

Mitch and I hung out in our hotel room that night after a workout that helped bring us back down to some normalcy after so much politics. We flew home the next day, and now it truly was decision time.

I went out to my backyard cabin office to think, and I actually broke down emotionally. I knew my answer, and both Karl Rove and the people in that Marshalltown Maid-Rite really helped me realize it: politics was not for me. I loved my family and wrestling too much to take this on. My backup, Mitch, confirmed this, so there was no split decision. I made the best decision I could for everyone and everything involved, and I still think it was the right one.

The Mirror

Looking into a mirror or self-reflecting every day is a way of seeing how you feel the important things are going in your life. If there isn't a mirror around, that's okay. It's not the visual reflection that matters anyway, but the mental check-in you do while looking at yourself. During that check-in, you ask yourself, "Am I in a good place right now? Do I need to make changes?" Based on that, you know if you need to stay on track or continue building daily to make positive changes.

One of my high school teachers and our assistant wrestling coach, Bill Blake, gave me a short book that he wrote in 1990 to reflect on his life. It was about his family and was written in memory of his dad. It was an interesting read, but toward the end, I finally absorbed the book's real meaning that broke me up: death doesn't end a relationship.

The book opens with a quote: "The future is no more than the present which resembles the past." Bill writes:

"For many years I pondered this quote to answer the questions of the future. I believe that people who have the skills and understanding to live and survive well in the present will carry those attributes into a successful future. The key to the future is then gaining the knowledge for a rewarding present. One of the ways to understand and appreciate the ever-present now is,

therefore, by looking at the past. By looking at the past, one will be able to better understand the present, which will carry me into the future."

I have read that passage again and again over the years, and it holds real meaning for me. It inspired my daily habit of reflecting and checking in with myself and seeing how I'm doing. By doing this every day, I know how I am feeling in the present. If I consistently feel that I am in a good place with my life, my profession, my family, and my health, then great! If not, then I know I need to reevaluate the past and make changes until the mirror, and my mind, reflects that I am in a good place in the present on a stable and consistent basis.

Making this daily self-evaluation gives me better knowledge of my past, and the responsibility of the future to get the current, ever-present now on track. It takes discipline, but I believe it is a vital part of effecting permanent, long-term change for the better.

28

The Gable Edge

In talking about having and cultivating an "edge," I would like to stick to the Gable Trained principle of simplicity and make it easy to understand and to accomplish. In reality, I can make it simple to understand what I did to develop an edge, but it is not actually easy to do. That's why this chapter is not short, like many in my first book and in this book. I feel the concepts are easy to follow, but the time, effort, and leadership needed to develop an edge are immense.

A lot goes into making a successful athlete and a complete person. It doesn't happen all at once, and it takes a lot of discipline and dedication. For me, it started when I was a kid, and I never really stopped or slowed down.

Television helped me understand the finer points of sports when I was in grade school. Before that, we only had the voice on the radio describing games and newspapers' reports of scores to inspire us. Now we could actually watch our sports heroes, which taught me so much about the individual sports and also motivated me to work harder and improve.

From the beginning, I had many sports heroes, such as pro-baseball player Mickey Mantle, pro-football player Jim Brown, and pro-basketball player Bob Cousy. I also had a lot of local wrestling heroes from East Waterloo and West Waterloo. There were a number of successful brother acts in wrestling in Waterloo, including the

Springers, the Buzzards, the Lanes, the Hoosmans, the Saddlers, and the Huffs. They all were champions, amassing some fifteen state wrestling titles at the high school level.

My sister was four years older than I was and often hung out with the wrestlers, so some of my local heroes often showed up at my house and had impromptu wrestling matches in my living room. Sometimes, they let me join in those matches, and I occasionally even got a cheer! That was a big deal for me, and it encouraged me to work even harder.

In addition to occasionally wrestling in our living room, I often played with or against my pro-athlete heroes in my mind. Imaginary football, baseball, and basketball games were always going on between the furniture and me. Swimming meets and flip turns on the walls were taking place in my head. I may have imagined myself going up against my sports heroes, but in reality I was actually swinging a bat, throwing pitches (usually rocks), running, throwing and kicking a football, or dribbling and shooting baskets. A lot of kids do this, and it's important because this training makes learning technique easier when it becomes real.

My family channeled this focus into positive locations like the YMCA or little league baseball. I played all kinds of sports through the YMCA: boxing, wrestling, basketball, swimming, and many others. Swimming was the first sport I really gravitated toward and did well in, winning the state and regional competitions.

Even this early in my athletic life, I took practices very seriously, and made sure to prepare myself thoroughly for them. Preparing for a real competition is pretty normal for everyone, but preparation for everyday practice was always in my mind. I even sometimes wrote notes to myself during class about the upcoming practice or event.

In junior high, I was on the football, wrestling, and baseball teams at my school. I was better at wrestling, but above-average at the others. There were organized basketball games every Saturday morning in the seventh grade. Before junior high, swimming had been my most successful sport, but I had to stop swimming competitively because it and wrestling were during the same season, so I had to choose one or the other. I picked the right one. In addition, in eighth grade, I really learned how to be a successful student academically, which actually helped my commitment to sports. It introduced even more discipline to my life.

During wrestling season in junior high, I sometimes checked myself out of study hall or library hour in the late morning to get in an extra training session. This usually involved rope skipping and some strength and conditioning exercises like chin-ups, push-ups, or sit-ups. If I could get a partner, we would get an extra wrestling session in. Then I would shower, grab lunch, and head back to my next class.

If I didn't get a ride home after school, I always ran home, even after sports practices. It was only just over a mile, but a lot of it was uphill. I always said that I was too lazy to walk home. It took too long! I thought walking was boring, and if I ran, I always got home quickly.

Almost daily after practices, I stopped at the local drugstore, which was right next to West Junior, to get a bottle of Nesbitt's orange soda. I would drink it there, and then either headed home by foot or was picked up by my sister or parents. It was almost a ritual, that drink. These days, it has changed to Mountain Dew. I know it's not the best habit, but I still enjoy it. In high school, the wrestlers had a drink we called "Burley Juice," which was a mixture of Gatorade and Mountain Dew. Coach Siddens, whom we called Burley Bob behind his back, always told us to keep the mix heavy on the Gatorade and to keep the Mountain Dew percentage low. I don't know if he checked the mix, but it was a reward for working hard. I guess it worked, because we were tough enough to almost always win.

I experienced having to make weight for the first time as a sopho-more in high school. It took a total family commitment with meals, and I avoided soda and sweets the entire season, but the weight did come off. As I improved and became more confident about making weight, I moved to just having sweets and soda in moderation year-round, rather than eliminating them entirely, and that seemed to work well. My friend Doug Moses couldn't adapt like that. Every year during the wrestling season, he was totally strict in his diet, but when the season was over, look out! He had to make up for all those months of discipline, I guess.

Coach Siddens knew I liked to get an extra workout in the morn-ing, and he felt he could trust me, so he gave me a key to the high school gym. After that, I went in every morning at 6:00 A.M. to run, lift weights, and drill before school. I also continued my junior high habit, and I signed out of study hall for an extra daily hour of training in the late morning. This way, these extra workouts were separated from my morning workout and after-school practice. The school personnel were understanding and supportive about my desire to train.

I was always the last one to leave practice, and then I would spend an extra long time recovering after practice, with lots of alter-nating between a hot whirlpool and a cold shower. After dinner with my family, I tackled my homework. If it was early in the week, I would also get a strength-training session in my basement, or I would do some hard running outside for two or three miles, or a combination of the two. Sometimes my dad went to the YMCA, and I would accompany him there for a workout and a steam. On nights when my mom went grocery shopping, I'd run to the market and shop with her, then either run back home or ride with her, depend-ing on how I felt. Toward the end of the week before a competition, I would rest in the evening instead of working out.

The interesting thing is that I could recuperate quickly, and so I wanted to do these things. My recovery methods worked well, but I didn't really understand how or why at that age. Between just the feeling of winning and taking the time to relax after practice, I was ready to do more. Never underestimate these two factors: the good feelings that come with being very successful and ending practices with relaxation, recuperation, and taking the time to analyze your performance in a relaxed, recovery-focused atmosphere.

When I moved on to college at Iowa State University in Ames, the structure was very conducive to learning how to break into the next level of competition. Also, for many of us, it was our first time being away from home. Living in the dorms with an assigned roommate was mandatory for first-year athletes. We only got three years of eligibility in those days, just like in high school, so the first year was really for us to adjust to this new world. The athletic and academic adjustment was fairly easy for me personally, being a homebody by inclination. But I was also homesick, so my parents and I wrote letters to each other daily to help with the adjustment.

Coach Nichols initially kept the freshmen separate from the varsity athletes, which also helped with the adjustment. It was less of a shock, and we got to work out with the varsity team after a few weeks. That first year also gave me time to adjust to and understand the academic college system, so by my second year I was able to put more focus on wrestling and still have time for homework.

Meeting with my academic advisor and discussing my personal schedule priorities were also really helpful. For example, I preferred having a two-hour open time in the morning to work out on my own, and I didn't want to have to hurry to afternoon practice. It was difficult to get the perfect schedule, but if more days worked out than not, it helped my goals and plans. I stuck to my formal schedule during my freshman year, but after that, wrestling determined what I did when. I couldn't miss workouts, whether they were the afternoon team ones or my own morning ones. Everyone has to set priorities that are in line with their own passions and goals for the rest of their lives. By this point, I was certain that wrestling was going to be my main profession in life. Yet I knew that academic courses could only help me in this, so I took classes like physics, geometry, leadership, nutrition, kinesiology, biology, counseling, and physical education. When I was growing up, people said there were the three Rs of education: reading, (w)riting, and (a)rithmetic. But for me, there were actually four Rs in education: reading, (w)riting, (a)rithmetic, and (w)restling.

So college was another step up in discipline and dedication. Even my walks to class turned into a chance to run, often while wearing ankle weights. People ask me now how I could do this without being embarrassed or worrying about people watching me. The answer is simple: it didn't faze me, as I was a man on a mission, and this was my path to achieve it. I never even thought about what other people thought of me at the time.

My recovery after our afternoon practices determined whether I could work out again that night. During my freshman year, I was able to more often than not, especially because we weren't competing as much as the varsity wrestlers. For me, this could mean boxing in my dorm room, pumping dumbbells that I brought from home, lifting weights in the dorm weight room, running the bleachers at the football stadium, doing hard running on the indoor track at the gym, or working out in the wrestling room. My morning workouts were mostly hard running and hard drilling with a partner, or shadow drilling by myself. I often did the hard drilling and hand fighting right after the hard running: remember, there is no jogging in a wrestling match. The pace is ferocious!

Even trips home to Waterloo with wrestling friends involved workouts at my house or at West High School where Bob Siddens was continuing to coach championship wrestling teams. Sometimes the wrestlers accompanying me simply enjoyed the comfort of my home and parents, or the social life of local kids our age, but for me, workouts were always included.

Things were moving along in my wrestling career as I hoped, but then, in my final college match, disaster struck: I lost. Losing to Larry Owings at the 1970 NCAA finals, my only loss in high school or college, could have been a major setback for me. It really hurt at the time, but in the end, I used it to become a better wrestler. After that loss, I critiqued myself more and implemented those critiques into my daily training. I needed to get better at scoring from standing positions and at defense. I started studying and analyzing the skills and tactics top international wrestlers used, since that was the direction I would be heading in next. That loss taught me that in addition to working hard in practice, I also needed to work smart.

After that, getting right back on the wrestling mat and having immediate success, both in practices and in competitions, were important in such a mental sport. It wasn't automatic, and I had to continue being more disciplined, both physically and mentally.

I was moving into international wrestling now, so a new level of excellence was expected if I was going to be successful. At the World championships in Edmonton, Canada, in late summer 1970, I was an alternate for US team member Bobby Douglas. I was a sponge for learning at that event, taking in as much as I could.

I continued to make headway in my training in late 1970 and early 1971. My focus now was smartness in training, which included exposing the shoulders of my opponents from all positions. That's how you score big points in international wrestling. In addition, making a name for yourself at this level with unique attributes or skills creates havoc amongst your top opponents, which I was able to do fairly quickly. Successfully wrestling against the Russians early on put me in a category of a select few, since they dominated the wrestling world at the time. They still do, in fact, except for in the female category, where Japan is the biggest powerhouse.

My training became practically full time in 1971 and 1972. I wasn't taking on summer jobs anymore and was fully focused on wrestling on a daily basis. I did still take graduate classes part-time during the traditional academic year though. Taking classes actually made me a better wrestler in some ways. They helped me understand people better, or understand different types of learning that can enhance performance. They also gave me another outlet to practice hard work and discipline so that I had something outside the wrestling room to keep me in that right mindset.

Even though I was training practically full time now in terms of the number of days and hours spent in the wrestling room, my mindset and focus had never really changed since as far back as I could remember. To this day, my mindset is the same, and all that changes is what my days consist of. No matter what I'm doing day-to-day, my mindset has always been on making my best effort, achieving my goals, continuing toward my passions, maintaining a healthy lifestyle, and making sure I take time for recovery to stay strong.

Once I had reached this point in my wrestling profession, it became as much about what I had to do on a daily basis to ready myself for competition as what I had to do to stay current with, or even ahead of, the larger world of wrestling. I never stopped training and working hard, but now there was more to it than that.

To better see what I mean, this is a list of many of the things I did within the larger sport, starting when I was in high school. It shows how important it is to go above and beyond the already established norm if you want to be very successful at anything.

1964 AND 1965

Attended weeklong summer wrestling camps at the University of Iowa along with my teammate and best friend, Doug Moses. I had some pretty good scrapes with others who attended.

1966

Attended summer Olympic Development Camp in Colorado for invited graduating high school seniors in the United States. I worked with Japanese Olympic and World champions in freestyle and Greco-Roman, including 1964 freestyle Olympic champion Yojiro Uetake and 1964 Greco-Roman Olympic champion Masamitsu Ichiguchi. Both gave me a lot of personal time and both impressed me immensely.

1967

Wrestled well in several unattached matches and tournaments, including the national freestyle championship. Went with Bob Buzzard to the Pan-American Games wrestling training camp in Minneapolis, Minnesota, during the summer and experienced new workout partners and training at a higher level of excellence.

1968

I went to the Olympic training camp for freestyle and Greco-Roman style wrestling at Adams State University in Alamosa, Colorado, for several weeks this summer and fall. I actually took a leave of absence from ISU and missed the whole first quarter of school. This was a monumental camp for me, and I probably got more out of it than any camp to date. It took me to a new level, and it helped put Tom Peckham on the Olympic team. I worked out with Wayne Wells, Bobby Douglas, Tom Huff, Rick Sanders, Werner Holzer, Steve Combs, and others. Olympic coach Tommy Evans, the head coach at the University of Oklahoma, took a special interest in me. I believe he liked my attitude and work ethic.

1969

In the spring, I competed at the national freestyle championships in Waterloo, Iowa, and won the tournament, but I didn't attend any summer camps. Looking back on it now, this may have been one of the reasons I did not win the 1970 NCAA championships the following year.

1970

I competed in and won the freestyle national championships three weeks after losing the 1970 NCAA finals match. I trained with the US World team in Duluth, Minnesota, for three weeks in the summer, and then attended the World championships in Edmonton, Canada. Not only did I help the United States prepare for that event, but I also helped us prepare for the future. Beyond attending our own training, I viewed as many of the foreign training practices as I could before the tournament. During the tournament, I followed many of the big-name wrestlers around before and after their matches—even walking into their locker rooms sometimes to see their reactions after a match. I also watched the Greco-Roman training and competitions.

1971

My first international tournament was the Tbilisi tournament in the Republic of Georgia, where I ended with a silver medal and learned a valuable lesson: don't get behind on the scoreboard, because you never know when the match will stop. Exact time was always shaky at international tournaments, because the clocks were often on the scorer's table and away from public view. This tournament also started my international following, because the fans really enjoyed my style of wrestling—though not to the extent that they wanted me to win. A month later I competed in four USSR–USA duals in Chattanooga, Oklahoma City, Waterloo, and Evanston. I was the only wrestler to wrestle in all four duals and ended up with one tie and three wins against the same Russian opponent, pinning him at our last stop. It provided a lot of valuable experience in a short period of time. It's hard to believe that I would wrestle four duals in a row, but it was an easy decision for me at that time. Myron Roderick was a smart coach and knew that I was a good draw in each city. He also recognized that I could be a potential star in the future. Next, tryouts for the Pan-American Games and the World championships were held at the same time at the US Naval Academy. If you won the trials, you were on both teams. I had two matches and won by a combined score of 50–0. We trained for a short period of time, and then went to Cali, Colombia, for the Pan-American Games. I had a tough final with my Cuban opponent until the third period. It was 2–2 after the second period, and I won 11–2. That Cuban ended up fourth at the World championships in Bulgaria a month later. After the Pan-American Games, we came back to the Naval Academy to finish training for the World championships. We trained in the Naval Academy armory and stayed in the locker room, where they had bunk beds set up for us. Everything was under one roof: mats, track, housing, locker rooms, sauna, etc. The World championships were in Sofia, Bulgaria, and we wrestled in an outdoor arena. The Soviet wrestler who beat me at the Tbilisi tournament earlier that year ended up second under a different bracketing system, and I beat him in the first round by a score of 5–1. I pinned three other opponents and disqualified a Turkish wrestler after leading 10–0 because he refused to finish the match against me. I wrestled a Bulgarian in the final match and beat him 8–3, winning the World championships.

1972

I won the Tbilisi tournament in January and won a bear coat for being named the Outstanding Wrestler of the tournament. We made two other stops in the Soviet Union for duals, and I won by a pin in both matches. I had a knee injury shortly after Tbilisi and missed some competitions. I entered the regional Olympic trials in Iowa

City, where I had six matches and six falls. I did not need to wrestle in this tournament since I was the reigning World champion, but I was testing my injured knee for competition instead of just practice. It held up well, but I was scoring more defensively than normal, which turned out to be a good thing, since it made me more of a complete wrestler. A few weeks later, we had the final Olympic trials in Anoka, Minnesota, which determined the lineup of participants from one through six. Lloyd Keaser came through the process to reach the finals, and we had to wrestle to the best two out of three. I beat Keaser, who won the World championships the next year, 22–0 and 11–0. Believe it or not, Lloyd was extremely competitive during those matches, which is what allowed me to score all those points. Next were the Olympic training and then the games themselves in Munich. I did not march in the opening ceremonies since our competition was early in the games. Standing and waiting were not conducive for competing. Years later, when I was the head freestyle Olympic wrestling coach at the 1984 Olympic Games in Los Angeles, I marched in the opening ceremonies. It was a good time, but not good enough to jeopardize winning.

1973
I was the assistant coach for the Tbilisi tournament trip in the Soviet Union. Coach Farrell talked me into one more freestyle match on stage inside Madison Square Garden as well. I wrestled against future wrestling great Pavel Pinigin. I won 12–2, even though he scored the first two points.

1974
With my individual competition career over, I was the assistant coach at the World championships in Istanbul, Turkey. The Soviet wrestler whom I competed against in 1971 and 1972 won the gold and immediately took off his shoes, indicating he was retiring. But

instead of leaving his shoes there, he picked them up and gave them to me matside. Leaving your shoes on the mat is an international tradition for wrestlers announcing their retirement. His giving me his shoes, instead of leaving them on the mat, showed the great respect he had for me.

1975

I was the assistant coach at the World championships at Minsk, in the Soviet Union, now capital of Belarus. The Soviet wrestler I beat in the final match of the Olympics, Ruslan Ashuraliyev, won the World championships at 163 pounds. He wasn't retiring, so he kept his shoes.

1976

I was the assistant coach for the freestyle Olympic team under head coach Wayne Baughman. It consumed six weeks of the summer. Kathy attended the Olympic Games with me in Montreal, Quebec. There were lots of family sacrifices that summer as we drove to Montreal and stayed in a fraternity house for several days.

1977

This was my first time as the head wrestling coach of the US World championship team, and my first World Cup team, which was in Toledo, Ohio. The World Cup is basically the top teams from the previous World championships, battling it out in a dual meet format. It was a very special event. The World championships were held in Lausanne, Switzerland; however, the team training camp was in Iowa City. This helped my marriage, as my wife was pregnant and due to have our first child during the World championships. At that event, Stan Dziedzic's championship victory at 163 pounds over Iran's Mansour Barzegar resulted in what might have been the most tired opponent I have ever witnessed. Fifteen minutes after the match, Barzegar was still lying on the floor in exhaustion. Dave Schultz's victory at the 1986 Goodwill Games over the Soviet Union's Adlan Variev, John Smith's win over Khaser Isaev of the Soviet Union at the same event, and Jordan Burroughs's win over Russia's Denis Tsargush at the 2011 World championships also contend for most-exhausted opponents at the end of a match. In all four cases, their opponents were strung out on the floor after their losses with unbelievable pain on their faces. I can remember some tired athletes after workouts at Iowa State. Many wrestlers at the University of Iowa and on Team USA were pushed to their limits as well. This was to prevent losses from exhaustion. It's okay to win and be exhausted, but you don't want to be beaten by your own exhaustion.

1977 UNITED STATES FREESTYLE WORLD WRESTLING TEAM (4TH PLACE)

114.5 pounds—Randal Miller
125.5 pounds—Jack Reinwand (3rd)
136.5 pounds—Jim Humphrey (2nd)
149.5 pounds—Chuck Yagla
163 pounds—Stan Dziedzic (1st)
180.5 pounds—Chris Campbell (5th)
198 pounds—Laurent Soucie
220 pounds—Mike McCready
HWT—John Bowlsby

1977 UNITED STATES FREESTYLE WORLD CUP WRESTLING TEAM (2ND PLACE)

105.5 pounds—Bobby Weaver (2nd)
114.5 pounds—James Haines (3rd)
125.5 pounds—Jack Reinwand (2nd)
136.5 pounds—Jim Humphrey (4th)

149.5 pounds—Chuck Yagla (2nd)

163 pounds—Stan Dziedzic (1st)

180.5 pounds—Wade Schalles (2nd)

198 pounds—Bud Palmer (2nd)

220 pounds—Harold Smith (2nd)

HWT—Jimmy Jackson (1st)

1978

This year I was the head wrestling coach for the US team at the freestyle World championships in Mexico City, Mexico, and head wrestling coach at the freestyle World Cup in Toledo, Ohio. One World champ, Stan Dziedzic, retired and another, Lee Kemp, took his place. I love having that depth in a team.

1978 UNITED STATES FREESTYLE WORLD WRESTLING TEAM (5TH PLACE)

105.5 pounds—William Rosado

114.5 pounds—James Haines (3rd)

125.5 pounds—Randy Lewis

136.5 pounds—Tim Cysewski

149.5 pounds—Jim Humphrey

163 pounds—Lee Kemp (1st)

180.5 pounds—John Peterson (3rd)

198 pounds—Ben Peterson (5th)

220 pounds—Larry Bielenberg (6th)

HWT—Greg Wojciechowski (5th)

1978 UNITED STATES FREESTYLE WORLD CUP WRESTLING TEAM (2ND PLACE)

105.5 pounds—Rich Salamone (2nd)

114.5 pounds—James Haines (1st)

125.5 pounds—Jack Reinwand (3rd)

136.5 pounds—Tim Cysewski (2nd)

149.5 pounds—Dave Schultz (2nd)

163 pounds—Wade Schalles (2nd)

180.5 pounds—Mark Lieberman (1st)

198 pounds—Laurent Soucie (2nd)

220 pounds—Russ Hellickson (1st)

HWT—Jimmy Jackson (1st)

1979

I was the head wrestling coach of the World championship team, which was held this year in San Diego, California, and of the World Cup in Toledo, Ohio. Between the summers of 1977–79, my wife, Kathy, and my daughters Jenni and Annie stayed with me in an apartment or in hotels in Colorado Springs, Colorado, the headquarters of USA Wrestling, for several weeks of training camp. It was a pretty big commitment for them, but the area had lots of fun family activities and sights for them to enjoy. How do you get seven medals and place second as a team? Russia and its continued excellence and dominance in wrestling are how.

1979 UNITED STATES FREESTYLE WORLD WRESTLING TEAM (2ND PLACE)

105.5 pounds—Bobby Weaver (2nd)

114.5 pounds—James Haines (2nd)

125.5 pounds—Joe Corso (3rd)

136.5 pounds—Andre Metzger (3rd)

149.5 pounds—Chuck Yagla

163 pounds—Lee Kemp (1st)

180.5 pounds—John Peterson (2nd)

198 pounds—Laurent Soucie (6th)

220 pounds—Russ Hellickson (2nd)

HWT—David Klemm

1979 UNITED STATES FREESTYLE WORLD CUP WRESTLING TEAM (2ND PLACE)

105.5 pounds—Bill Rosado (2nd)

114.5 pounds—Mike McArthur (4th)

125.5 pounds—Jack Reinwand (2nd)

136.5 pounds—Tim Cysewski (1st)

149.5 pounds—Chuck Yagla (1st)

163 pounds—Lee Kemp (1st)

180.5 pounds—Mark Lieberman (2nd)

198 pounds—Ben Peterson (2nd)

220 pounds—Fred Bohna (2nd)

HWT—Jimmy Jackson (1st)

1980

I was set to be the head freestyle wrestling coach of the 1980 Olympic team, but the US boycotted the summer Olympics in Moscow due to the Soviet Union's invasion of Afghanistan. This team was ready to win in Moscow if they had been able to attend the games. The US decision to boycott caused much debate and heartbreak for many, but there were also definitely lessons learned for some. I was also the head wrestling coach for the freestyle World Cup team in Toledo, Ohio.

1980 UNITED STATES FREESTYLE OLYMPIC WRESTLING TEAM (BOYCOTTED)

105.5 pounds—Bobby Weaver

114.5 pounds—Gene Mills

125.5 pounds—John Azevedo

136.5 pounds—Randy Lewis

149.5 pounds—Chuck Yagla

163 pounds—Lee Kemp

180.5 pounds—Chris Campbell

198 pounds—Ben Peterson
220 pounds—Russ Hellickson
HWT—Greg Wojciechowski

1980 UNITED STATES FREESTYLE WORLD CUP WRESTLING TEAM (1ST PLACE)

105.5 pounds—Bobby Weaver (1st)
114.5 pounds—Gene Mills (1st)
125.5 pounds—Nick Gallo (2nd)
136.5 pounds—Andre Metzger (2nd)
149.5 pounds—Dave Schultz (1st)
163 pounds—Lee Kemp (1st)
180.5 pounds—John Peterson (1st)
198 pounds—Ben Peterson (1st)
220 pounds—Larry Bielenberg (2nd)
HWT—Jimmy Jackson (1st)

1981

This year, I was a volunteer coach for the freestyle World championship team in Skopje, Yugoslavia, and head wrestling coach for the freestyle World Cup team in Toledo, Ohio. I also went to Japan to coach the World super championships. Former Hawkeye Chris Campbell won the World championships. Coaching three major international events, plus attending national USA Wrestling events at different age groups and levels, along with my normal work at Iowa caused me to really focus on great leadership and taught me how to delegate many duties.

1981 UNITED STATES FREESTYLE WORLD CUP WRESTLING TEAM (2ND PLACE)

105.5 pounds—Bobby Weaver (2nd)
114.5 pounds—Gene Mills (1st)

125.5 pounds—Ricky Dellagatta (3rd)

136.5 pounds—Andre Metzger (3rd)

149.5 pounds—Dave Schultz (2nd)

163 pounds—Lee Kemp (1st)

180.5 pounds—Chris Campbell (1st)

198 pounds—Howard Harris (2nd)

220 pounds—Greg Gibson (2nd)

HWT—Jimmy Jackson (2nd)

1982

I was a volunteer coach for the freestyle World championships held in Edmonton, Canada, and head coach for the freestyle World Cup team in Toledo, Ohio. I loved going to Toledo for the World Cup. The media coverage was phenomenal, as was the hospitality. Local wrestling legends Dick Torio, Joe Scalzo, and Greg Wojciechowski were often in attendance as well.

1982 UNITED STATES FREESTYLE WORLD CUP WRESTLING TEAM (1ST PLACE)

105.5 pounds—Adam Cuestas (1st)

114.5 pounds—Joe Gonzales (1st)

125.5 pounds—Gene Mills (2nd)

136.5 pounds—Randy Lewis (2nd)

149.5 pounds—Andy Rein (2nd)

163 pounds—Lee Kemp (1st)

180.5 pounds—Mark Schultz (1st)

198 pounds—Howard Harris (2nd)

220 pounds—Greg Gibson (2nd)

HWT—Bruce Baumgartner (2nd)

1983

I was the head coach for the freestyle World championships held in Kiev, Soviet Union, and the head wrestling coach for the freestyle World Cup team in Toledo, Ohio. Upon arriving in Kiev, we learned that, surprisingly, the rules of wrestling had been changed—and we were unaware of the new changes. Mat wrestling was being more heavily emphasized than previously. We adapted and we still did okay.

1983 UNITED STATES FREESTYLE WORLD WRESTLING TEAM (3RD PLACE)

105.5 pounds—Bobby Weaver (5th)
114.5 pounds—Joe Gonzales
125.5 pounds—Barry Davis
136.5 pounds—Lee Roy Smith (2nd)
149.5 pounds—Nate Carr
163 pounds—Dave Schultz (1st)
180.5 pounds—Mark Schultz
198 pounds—Ed Banach
220 pounds—Greg Gibson (2nd)
HWT—Bruce Baumgartner (3rd)

1983 UNITED STATES FREESTYLE WORLD CUP WRESTLING TEAM (2ND PLACE)

105.5 pounds—Adam Cuestas (1st)
114.5 pounds—Joe Gonzales (2nd)
125.5 pounds—Gene Mills (2nd)
136.5 pounds—Lee Roy Smith (2nd)
149.5 pounds—Nate Carr (2nd)
163 pounds—Dave Schultz (2nd)
180.5 pounds—Chris Campbell (1st)
198 pounds—Mitch Hull (3rd)

220 pounds—Harold Smith (2nd)

HWT—Bruce Baumgartner (2nd)

1984

I was the head coach for the US teams at the Tbilisi tournament in the USSR, the World Cup in Toledo, Ohio, and the Olympic Games in Los Angeles, California. We trained in Colorado and Big Bear, California, for eight weeks, accompanied by my family. Our freestyle wrestling team was voted the best US Olympic team performance at the games. The United States also won its first Olympic gold medals in Greco-Roman wrestling with Steve Fraser (198 pounds) and Jeff Blatnick (HWT).

1984 UNITED STATES FREESTYLE OLYMPIC WRESTLING TEAM (SEVEN GOLD, TWO SILVER)

105.5 pounds—Bobby Weaver (1st)

114.5 pounds—Joe Gonzales

125.5 pounds—Barry Davis (2nd)

136.5 pounds—Randy Lewis (1st)

149.5 pounds—Andy Rein (2nd)

163 pounds—Dave Schultz (1st)

180.5 pounds—Mark Schultz (1st)

198 pounds—Ed Banach (1st)

220 pounds—Lou Banach (1st)

HWT—Bruce Baumgartner (1st)

1984 UNITED STATES FREESTYLE WORLD CUP WRESTLING TEAM (2ND PLACE)

105.5 pounds—Bobby Weaver (1st)

114.5 pounds—Joe Gonzales (1st)

125.5 pounds—Mike Land (2nd)

136.5 pounds—Lee Roy Smith (2nd)

149.5 pounds—Lennie Zalesky (2nd)

163 pounds—Lee Kemp and Mike DeAnna

180.5 pounds—Chris Campbell (1st)

198 pounds—Ed Banach (2nd)

220 pounds—Greg Gibson (2nd)

HWT—Bruce Baumgartner (1st)

1985

I was a volunteer assistant coach for the World championship team in Budapest, Hungary, this year. The new head coach of Oklahoma State, Joe Seay, was the head coach for the World team, and he led the United States to a third-place team finish, with Mark Schultz (180.5 pounds) and Bill Scherr (198 pounds) winning gold medals. Mike Houck (198 pounds) became the first wrestler from the United States to win a World championship in Greco-Roman wrestling.

1986

I was again a volunteer assistant coach for the World championships, which were in Budapest, Hungary. We earned seven medals, but we still came in second to the USSR. Jim Humphrey was the new US coach, and Bruce Baumgartner (HWT) won gold.

1987

I served as a volunteer assistant coach for the World championships in Clermont-Ferrand, France. We earned eight medals this year, but the USSR still won the gold medal as a team. John Smith (136.5 pounds) and Mark Schultz (180.5 pounds) won gold medals. The women's World wrestling championships started this year and were held in Norway, but the United States did not attend.

1988

I was an assistant coach for the US freestyle Olympic team that competed in Seoul, South Korea, and spent four weeks at training camp with the team. The United States won five freestyle medals, with John Smith (136.5 pounds) and Kenny Monday (163 pounds) from Oklahoma State bringing home the gold.

1989

I was again a volunteer assistant coach for the World championships in Martigny, Switzerland. The men's freestyle team earned six medals with Smith and Monday winning gold again. We also won four silver medals: Jim Scherr (198 pounds), Bill Scherr (220 pounds), Melvin Douglas (180.5 pounds), and Bruce Baumgartner (HWT). Bobby Douglas took over as head coach this year. The United States also attended its first World championships in women's freestyle wrestling. Afsoon Johnston (103.5 pounds) placed third, Asia DeWeese (110 pounds) placed second, and Leia Kawaii (154 pounds) placed second. These were our first three World medalists in women's wrestling.

1990

I attended the World championships in Tokyo, Japan, as a spectator and was the head coach of the freestyle World Cup team in Toledo, Ohio. We had five medals with Smith winning gold and two Hawkeyes—Royce Alger at 180.5 pounds and Chris Campbell at 198 pounds—with silvers. Baumgartner also picked up a silver medal, and Kirk Trost (220 pounds) picked up a bronze. Joe Wells, my first roommate at the University of Iowa, was the head coach.

1990 UNITED STATES FREESTYLE WORLD CUP WRESTLING TEAM (1ST PLACE)

105.5 pounds—Tim Vanni (2nd)

114.5 pounds—Eddie Woodburn (3rd)

125.5 pounds—Brad Penrith (3rd)

136.5 pounds—John Fisher (5th) and Greg Randall

149.5 pounds—John Giura (1st)

163 pounds—Rob Koll (3rd)

180.5 pounds—Melvin Douglas (3rd)

198 pounds—Jim Scherr (2nd)

220 pounds—Bill Scherr (1st)

HWT—Bruce Baumgartner (1st)

1991

I did not attend the World championships in Varna, Bulgaria, this year, but I followed the results. The United States won six medals again, with Smith's fifth straight gold. Zeke Jones (114.5 pounds) won gold by beating the great Valentin Jordanov in his home country, and Kevin Jackson (180.5 pounds) won as well.

1992

I did not attend the Olympics in Barcelona, Spain, but I did watch coverage from a dorm room in Mason City, Iowa, at North Iowa Area Community College while attending a youth wrestling camp. I watched all of the wrestling matches on a television during the middle of the night. My wife, Kathy, was somewhat annoyed by this, but she understood, and I turned the volume down so I wouldn't disturb her. Coach Bobby Douglas brought home six Olympic medalists, with John Smith winning his sixth straight gold, Jackson winning a second gold, and Baumgartner winning a third gold out of his ten medals. Jones, Monday, and Campbell were the other medalists. Greco-Roman wrestling had two medalists, with Rodney Smith

(149.5 pounds) winning bronze and Dennis Koslowski (220 pounds) winning silver. Although women's wrestling was not in the Olympics yet, Tricia Saunders became our first World champion by winning the 110-pound weight class in Villeurbanne, France.

1993

I was a volunteer on the coaching staff for the World championships in Toronto, Canada. The USSR was now Russia, and all the other Soviet republics were their own countries now as well. This shook up the international wrestling scene a great deal, and the USA finally won the freestyle men's title! Coached by Joe Seay and Bruce Burnett, and led by four gold medalists—Terry Brands (125.5 pounds), Tom Brands (136.5 pounds), Melvin Douglas (198 pounds), and Bruce Baumgartner—along with Dave Schultz's silver, this put the USA on top.

1994

I was the head freestyle wrestling coach for the World championships in Istanbul, Turkey. This was the second straight year that a team removed from the former Communist regime won. This time, it was Turkey. The Russians were scratching their heads but taking it seriously. The United States only came away with two medals this year. It was a rough tournament, and I learned some important lessons (see chapter 22 on the 1997 Iowa season).

1994 UNITED STATES FREESTYLE WORLD WRESTLING TEAM (9TH PLACE)

105.5 pounds—Tim Vanni (9th)
114.5 pounds—Zeke Jones
125.5 pounds—Terry Brands
136.5 pounds—Tom Brands
149.5 pounds—Townsend Saunders

163 pounds—Dave Schultz (7th)

180.5 pounds—Kevin Jackson

198 pounds—Melvin Douglas (3rd)

220 pounds—Mark Kerr

286 pounds—Bruce Baumgartner (2nd)

1995

I was a volunteer assistant coach for the freestyle World champion-ships held in Atlanta, Georgia, and was the head coach for the free-style World Cup in Chattanooga, Tennessee. This was the third year in a row that the title escaped Russia. The United States team won gold. There were lots of politics this year, but the USA had a very good team of athletes and coaches. Terry Brands (125.5 pounds), Kevin Jackson (180.5 pounds), Kurt Angle (220 pounds), and Bruce Baumgartner (286 pounds) won gold medals. Zeke Jones was on a tear, but because the Americans were dominating, he paid the price. He placed third but should have won the gold. The officials reversed one of his wins to a loss after a video review. This was not the first and certainly not the last time that this would happen. Dennis Hall also made history by becoming the second wrestler from the United States to win a World title in Greco-Roman wres-tling, at 125.5 pounds.

1995 UNITED STATES FREESTYLE WORLD CUP WRESTLING TEAM (1ST PLACE)

105.5 pounds—Tim Vanni (5th)

114.5 pounds—Zeke Jones (1st)

125.5 pounds—Terry Brands (1st)

136.5 pounds—Tom Brands (1st)

149.5 pounds—Brian Dolph (4th)

163 pounds—Dave Schultz (1st)

180.5 pounds—Kevin Jackson (1st)

198 pounds—Dominic Black (1st)
220 pounds—Kurt Angle (2nd)
HWT—Bruce Baumgartner (2nd)

1996

I was a volunteer assistant coach for the freestyle Olympic team in Atlanta, Georgia. I finally achieved my goal of passing out from working hard, but it took watching someone else wrestle, instead of participating myself. I actually passed out during one of Tom Brands's tough matches. This had almost happened once before during the 1991 NCAA tournament finals at 158 pounds between Tom Ryan and Oklahoma State's Pat Smith, but I held up. With Brands, I woke up in the training room in Atlanta. Brands (136.5 pounds), Kendall Cross (125.5 pounds), and Kurt Angle (220 pounds) all won gold medals. On the Greco-Roman side, we had three silvers: Brandon Paulson (114.5 pounds), Dennis Hall (125.5 pounds), and Matt Ghaffari (286 pounds). Tricia Saunders won her second World championship.

1997

I did not attend the freestyle World championships held in Krasnoyarsk, Russia, this year, but I followed it at home. The Russians were back on top in freestyle. The USA team only brought home two medals, with Les Gutches (187.25 pounds) winning gold and Cary Kolat (138.75 pounds) winning silver.

1998

I was a volunteer assistant coach for the freestyle World championships in Tehran, Iran. It was in a big arena, and all fifteen thousand–plus seats were sold out. The Iranians love wrestling. Sammie Henson (119 pounds) won gold and also won over the Iranian fans by complimenting them. Tricia Saunders (101.25 pounds) won her third World championship.

1999

I was the co-head coach, along with John Smith and Greg Strobel, for the freestyle World championships in Ankara, Turkey. Bruce Burnett was still overseeing the staff to keep us honest. The new pairing rules were crazy, which led to wrestlers wanting to lose in the first round so they could wrestle back, except for the very few who thought they could win. It was a real joke, and at that point, I knew wrestling was in trouble. Stephen Neal (286 pounds) won gold with his penetrating takedowns and by wearing his opponents down. Tricia Saunders won her fourth and final World championship.

1999 UNITED STATES FREESTYLE WORLD WRESTLING TEAM (2ND PLACE)

119 pounds—Eric Akin
127.75 pounds—Eric Guerrero (7th)
138.75 pounds—Cary Kolat (4th)
152 pounds—Lincoln McIlravy (2nd)
167.5 pounds—Joe Williams (4th)
187.25 pounds—Les Gutches (3rd)
213.75 pounds—Dominic Black
286 pounds—Stephen Neal (1st)

2000

I was again a co-head coach with John Smith and Greg Strobel, this time for the freestyle Olympic team in Sydney, Australia. We had six wrestlers in the semifinals and were on a roll, but the semifinals were our demise, and that brought us back down to earth. I almost saw it coming, but it was too late at this point. We left Sydney with no gold medals, but Slay won the gold medal that was rightfully his later because his German finals opponent failed a drug test. Henson won silver. Terry and Lincoln showed up strong enough to come away with bronze medals, though Terry could barely walk away.

Still, he wrestled enough to win. The biggest bang this year was in Greco-Roman wrestling, when Rulon Gardner beat the all-time Russian star, Alexander Karelin, a twelve-time World and Olympic champion, in the finals at super heavyweight. By doing so, he was a star at the 2000 Olympics.

2000 UNITED STATES FREESTYLE OLYMPIC WRESTLING TEAM (ONE GOLD, ONE SILVER, TWO BRONZE)

119 pounds—Sammie Henson (2nd)

127.75 pounds—Terry Brands (3rd)

138.75 pounds—Cary Kolat

152 pounds—Lincoln McIlravy (3rd)

167.5 pounds—Brandon Slay (1st)

187.25 pounds—Charles Burton (5th)

213.75 pounds—Melvin Douglas

286 pounds—Kerry McCoy (5th)

2001

The World championships were originally scheduled for New York City this year, but they were moved to Sofia, Bulgaria, after the events of 9/11 stunned the world. I did not attend. Our men's freestyle team had two medalists: Joe Williams (167.5 pounds) won a bronze and Brandon Eggum (187.25 pounds) won a silver. Rulon Gardner solidified his Olympic win with a World gold.

2002

The United States did not attend the freestyle World championships in Tehran, Iran, this year due to a credible threat of violence against the team. The United States was still struggling with security and safety in the wake of 9/11 the previous year. Dremiel Byers won a

Greco-Roman World championship (264.5 pounds), which was the third super heavyweight title in a row for the United States.

2003

The World championships that were originally scheduled for New York City in 2001 finally returned to New York City in 2003 and were held in Madison Square Garden. It was a good event for our country and for wrestling. The country of Georgia won, and the United States placed second, with Iran coming in third and Russia coming in fourth. Cael Sanderson (185 pounds) and Kerry McCoy (264.5 pounds) won silver medals. Kristie Davis won a gold medal in women's freestyle wrestling at 147.5 pounds. I attended these World championships as a spectator, and also coached my eleventh and final World Cup team in Boise, Idaho. I had a good run with the World Cups that I coached: of the eleven teams I coached, we had four team championships. World Cups had very little team training, but the athletes seemed to adapt quickly for competition.

2003 UNITED STATES FREESTYLE WORLD CUP WRESTLING TEAM (1ST PLACE)
121 pounds—Stephen Abas (1st)
132 pounds—Eric Guerrero (1st)
145.5 pounds—Chris Bono (1st)
163 pounds—Joe Williams (1st)
185 pounds—Cael Sanderson (2nd)
211.5 pounds—Tim Hartung (1st)
264.5 pounds—Kerry McCoy (3rd)

2004

I attended the Olympic Games in Athens, Greece, as a spectator. The United States won three medals in freestyle wrestling, with

Cael Sanderson (185 pounds) winning gold and Stephen Abas (121 pounds) and Jamill Kelly (145.5 pounds) with silvers. Rulon Gardner added a bronze medal in Greco-Roman wrestling to his list of World medals and left his wrestling shoes in the middle of the mat to signify his retirement. Women wrestled in the Olympics for the first time this year, and Team USA started their Olympic medal count with a silver, Sara McMann at 138.75 pounds, and a bronze, Patricia Miranda at 105.5 pounds. The women only had four weight classes initially, but moved up to be even with men's freestyle in 2016.

2005

I attended the World championships in Budapest, Hungary, as a spectator. There were two Iowa connections in bronze medalists Joe Williams (163 pounds) from the University of Iowa and Tolly Thompson (264.5 pounds) from Janesville, Iowa. Iris Smith won a gold medal in women's freestyle at 158.75 pounds. The women won the bronze team trophy under head coach Terry Steiner.

2006–2009

I did not attend the World championships or the Olympic Games during these years, but I followed them online. It is good to follow this level of competition from afar, but it was not the same as being there. The Zadick brothers, Bill and Mike, both won World medals. Bill (145.5 pounds) won gold and Mike (132 pounds) won silver. In Greco-Roman wrestling, the combination of University of Michigan graduates Steve Fraser, head national team coach for Greco-Roman, and Joe Warren, World champion in 2006, had a blueprint between the coach and athlete to make a big impact. Somehow, that blueprint got tarnished, leading to less spectacular results than what could have been. During this time, the United States won the Greco-Roman team title in 2007, but there could have been more individual and team titles. At the 2008 Olympics in Beijing, China, the United States earned three medals, led by Henry Cejudo winning a gold medal at 121 pounds in men's freestyle wrestling. The women had separate World championships in 2008 because of limited weight classes at the Olympics. Clarissa Chun won a World title at 105.5 pounds. It was a lean year for the US in 2009, with two medals: silvers for Jake Herbert at 185 pounds in freestyle and Dremiel Byers at 264.5 pounds in Greco-Roman.

2010

I attended the World championships in Moscow, Russia, as a spectator. There wasn't much to cheer about on the men's side of things, with no medals in Greco-Roman or freestyle. On the women's side, there were two medals: Tatiana Padilla (121 pounds) won a bronze medal and Elena Pirozhkova (138.75 pounds) was a silver medalist.

2011

I did not attend the World championships in Istanbul, Turkey, but I followed the matches online. Jordan Burroughs (163 pounds) won his first World championship by stopping Denis Tsargush's string of three World titles. Former Iowa State wrestler Jake Varner (211.5 pounds) won a bronze medal and brought Iowa's medal count up a notch.

2012

I attended the 2012 Olympics in London, England, as a spectator with my wife, Kathy, and my youngest daughter, Mackie. During the freestyle competition, I was inducted into the FILA International Wrestling Hall of Fame in the Legends category. As of 2016, only five wrestlers have been inducted into this category. Jordan Burroughs led the way for the US Olympic team with a gold medal at 163 pounds. Jake Varner topped it off by becoming Iowa State University's sixth Olympic gold medalist, and he was the final gold medalist of the 2012 Olympic wrestling competition. Coleman Scott (132 pounds) fought to the end to win a bronze medal. The women had another stand-alone World championship event, with Elena Pirozhkova (138.75 pounds) and Adeline Gray (158.5 pounds) winning gold medals. Clarissa Chun (105.5 pounds) won a bronze medal at the Olympics.

2013

I attended the World championships in Budapest, Hungary, as a spectator. Jordan Burroughs was the highlight of the event again, winning his third World and Olympic titles in a row. It was a rough year for the guys, but the women were holding their own with a bronze team medal and three individual bronze medalists for Alyssa Lampe, Elena Pirozhkova, and Adeline Gray. The world of wrestling spent a lot of its time in Budapest working for the future of wrestling after the International Olympic Committee's recommendation to drop wrestling from the Olympics. Shortly after Budapest, our six months of working together gave wrestling a first-round voting win to reinstate wrestling back into the Olympics, with plenty of work to go to stabilize that decision. The United States formed a committee called the Committee to Preserve Olympic Wrestling (CPOW), which spent many hours helping coordinate the effort to get reinstated. Led by 1985 World champion Bill Scherr, with direction from Stan Dziedzic, the vice president of our international governing body, United World Wrestling, and Rich Bender, executive director of USA Wrestling, the committee had lots of energy and finances to help the total process work successfully. Another example of working together and winning together! Being an active member of CPOW, I traveled nonstop and was interviewed daily during this threatening period. In Iowa, Governor Branstad led the governors of the United States in showing support for the initiative of reinstatement. He was a great help.

2014

I did not attend the World championships in Tashkent, Uzbekistan, but I followed them online. Jordan Burroughs (163 pounds) injured his leg in the first round, lost to the Russian, Tsargush, but came back and won the bronze. Tervel Dlagnev (275 pounds) earned a bronze in men's freestyle, and Andy Bisek (165 pounds) earned a bronze in Greco-Roman, our first medal in Greco since 2009. Adeline Gray (165 pounds) won her second World gold.

2015

I attended the World championships in Las Vegas, Nevada, as a spectator and a promoter. This was the first time the United States hosted the World championships since 2003. We took a chance by holding the event in Las Vegas, given that we needed this tournament to run smoothly since the reinstatement of wrestling at the Olympics was still recent. Thankfully, everything did go smoothly. The United States ended with seven medals, highlighted by Jordan Burroughs (163 pounds) winning his fourth World and Olympic titles, Kyle Snyder (213 pounds) becoming the youngest World champion in US history, Helen Maroulis (121 pounds) winning her first World championship, and Adeline Gray (165 pounds) winning her third. We also came away with bronze medals from James Green (154 pounds) in men's freestyle, Andy Bisek (165 pounds) in Greco-Roman, and Leigh Jaynes-Provisor (132 pounds) in women's freestyle.

2016

With lots of controversy from the media going into the Rio Olympic Games, I wasn't planning on attending. In addition, the coverage from NBC was at its highest, and there were four major channels broadcasting the Olympics, plus online. A few weeks prior to the start of the Olympics, I received a call from Nick Gallo of ASICS

America and TW Promotions, asking me to go to Rio on their behalf. I pondered this in detail, but with my wife recovering from a fall (not on the wrestling mat), I decided to go with the best approach: stay home, take care of Kathy, and follow the games closely on all the networks. In reality, watching the entire Olympics provided a better perspective about the sport of wrestling. Without dwelling on all the details, the attention paid to wrestling is over and done with much too quickly, due to our competition rules where they must complete one weight class in a day. It made me think back to my five days of competition in Munich at the 1972 Olympics and how much exposure our sport received over five days compared to a one-day event. In my role of promoting the sport, I felt like staying home and watching all of the sports gave me more insight into what is needed in wrestling. The future of the sport depends on women's wrestling, and the top leadership of our international governing body needs to know this. From USA Wrestling's point of view, our first gold medal in women's freestyle wrestling was definitely a highlight. Helen Maroulis's win over Saori Yoshida in the 116.5-pound finals was a monumental upset. Yoshida was a sixteen-time World and Olympic champion who was going for her fourth Olympic gold medal. On the men's freestyle side, two current college wrestlers earned medals for the United States: Kyle Snyder, at 213 pounds, became the youngest Olympic wrestling champion in US history by winning the gold medal at the age of twenty, and J'Den Cox won a bronze at 189 pounds. Both were still in college at the time, which is positive news for the future of wrestling in our country.

Former Iowa wrestlers Daniel Dennis and Tony Ramos faced each other in the finals of the Olympic trials in Iowa City for the 125.5-pound spot on the freestyle wrestling Olympic team. Dennis, an NCAA tournament finalist in 2010, made the team over two-time World team member and 2014 NCAA champion Ramos.

United World Wrestling wisely held a World championship in

December for all non-Olympic weight classes (two for men's freestyle, two for women's freestyle, and two for men's Greco-Roman). Logan Stieber, a four-time NCAA champion for Ohio State, was a World champion at 134 pounds in men's freestyle while Alli Ragan earned a silver medal at 132 pounds in women's freestyle.

■ ■ ■

As you can tell from reading that list, there are a number of things that can help your performance beyond just your work with your own team. It is necessary to stay current at the highest level of your profession. It is easier to follow events through the Internet today, but that doesn't replace the first-hand experience of being on-site, though it does help and is very good.

There is one final key to my success that I want to remember: family. The commitment of having a family can make it difficult to balance priorities, but I have seen again and again that those wrestlers who do not have the strong support and backing of their family have a much harder time. I'm not saying that they can't do well at the highest levels of the sport, just that having your family supporting you can make many things easier and often more worthwhile.

Growing up, I had a lot of help and support from my parents and sister, and this continued when I grew up and started a family of my own. While it did increase my responsibilities, it just meant I had that many more people cheering for me. Never slight the focus on your personal life, or it will affect your total life, and most likely not in positive ways.

When you take the time to analyze what is working well and why, then you should stay within those parameters for continued success or to get back to that success level.

The family connections have been a mainstay over the years in more ways than you can imagine. They have been consistent and powerful with the results as proof, yet they have helped show the directions needed when the results are less than desired. The Brands, Steiner, and Streicher families brought us back in our biggest drought. But before and after, there have been so many connections directly to the program. It definitely makes a difference, for the proof is there, yet this is but one of the important factors for great performance. Remember, it's not just the competitor connections; it actually goes into all the connections needed for the total success of the program or even the whole school. Look at the Carver name and how that name affected not just the wrestling program but the entire school.

The strength in the numbers of names has contributed a great deal to wrestling's overall success through the years. I'll give you some examples before, during, and even after my years:

Andersons, Ballwegs, Banachs, Bowlsbys, Brandses, Buraks, Chiapparellis, DeAnnas, Dressers, Eustices, Evanshevskises, Fulsaasses, Gillmors, Glenns, Glynns, Guernseys, Hands, Happels, Hatchers, Heffernans, Heyings, Hruskas, Huffs, Ironsides, Juergenses, Kauffmans, Kellys, Kemps, Kistlers, Kurdelmeiers, LeCleres, Lepics, Levys, Loeras, Lofthouses, McCanns, McGinnesses, McGiverns, Meyers, Moccos, Moores, Morkels, Mosers, Muellers, Novaks, O'Learys, Papes, Pfeffers, Randalls, Robertses, Ryans, Schwabs, Senneffs, Shermans, Smiths, Stanleys, Stearnses, Stedmans, Steiners, Stevensons, St. Johns, Streichers, Strittmatters, Strubs, Trizzinos, Turks, Ukers, Webers, Wellses, Whitmers, Wilkersons, Williamses, Yaglas, Yegges, Zadicks, Zaleskys, Zaputils.

Many family names to list, of course not all, but it has worked well. Just one more piece of the puzzle that helps you to successful completions.

The edge I'm talking about isn't always just a slight one. All of these edges over time can lead to big differences, which can lead to more-than-slight wins and to record performances and domination.

25 Years of All-Americans and Big Ten Champions in My Words, 1973–1997

In my first season as an assistant coach with the Hawkeyes (1973), a sleeper (no, not Mark Stevenson!), Fred Penrod (190 pounds), just decided to step up, wrestle extremely hard, and win the Big Ten championship. Jan Sanderson (158 pounds) stopped his knitting and captured one too, but then went back to his knitting. Dan Sherman (118 pounds) decided to shut me up for all the yelling I did at him, especially at the end of practices, and captured a Big Ten title as well. Two of these three ended their seasons below the top of the podium. The exception was Dan Sherman, who went all the way and finished as a national champion. He really was tired of hearing me yell, and boy, did he shut me up! Dan Holm (150 pounds) finished his sophomore year with an NCAA third-place finish, surprising a few, but not me.

In 1974, a new name, Chris Campbell, immediately made an impact by winning the Big Tens. Sanderson repeated his previous year's performance, but at a weight higher (167 pounds). Chris Sones took over Dan Sherman's Big Ten top spot at 118 pounds. Sones didn't follow in Sherman's footsteps at the NCAAs, but Sanderson stepped up and went from sixth place to third. Holm repeated his 1973 placement with another bronze at the NCAAs. Chuck Yagla (150 pounds), from my hometown of Waterloo, Iowa, placed fourth.

The year 1975 was tough for Big Ten champions from Iowa, for only Chuck Yagla got the crown. Chuck used his riding skills and his seat belt hip move to control his way to the NCAA championship as well. But the Hawks had some other firepower that year. Dan Holm (158 pounds) stepped up and arm-barred his way to NCAA gold. Chris Campbell (177 pounds) lost a close battle in the NCAA finals to a tough opponent, Mike Lieberman of Lehigh, who came from behind to win. Greg Stevens (190 pounds) used a headlock to get himself in the finals, but also finished second to Iowa State's Al Nacin. Freshman John Bowlsby (HWT) finished third and helped the University of Iowa capture its first NCAA wrestling championship.

In **1976**, Chris Campbell returned to the top of the Big Tens and won his first NCAA title. In close matches, Chris was hard to stop near the end because of his explosiveness. Bud Palmer (190 pounds) and his famous leg sweep captured his first Big Ten title and finished third at the NCAAs. Yagla picked up his second Big Ten title, as well as his second gold at the NCAAs, and was also named the Outstanding Wrestler of the NCAAs the same year. John Bowlsby redshirted and played football that year, but another footballer-wrestler stepped in and finished fifth as an All-American: Waverly, Iowa's Doug Benschoter, a tough-nosed competitor who threw me into a pool at the celebration after. Tim Cysewski (134 pounds), Dan Wagemann (167 pounds), and Brad Smith (142 pounds) finished third, second, and first, respectively. It was quite an evening for Brad, who set himself apart with a major win. Also, both Cysewski and Wagemann finished about as close as one could get!

My first year as head coach, **1977**, had several new kids in the lineup. We had five Big Ten champions, but we stumbled at the NCAAs outside our five All-Americans. Interestingly, we had a first (Campbell at 177 pounds), a second (Mourlam at 126 pounds), a third (DeAnna at 167 pounds), a fourth (McGivern at 158 pounds), and a fifth (Bowlsby at heavyweight). Chris Campbell won his third Big Ten title this year, as well as his second NCAA title, and went on to be a World champion. Not bad for being a recruiting surprise!

My first outright championship happened in **1978**, and it was a close one, by only half a point over ISU, but we had a lot of youngsters with the right attitude. Many of them were entertainers on the mat with their attitude and style. John Bowlsby won his second Big Ten title, and picked up his third All-Americanship. Mike DeAnna also won his second Big Ten, and became an All-American again. Fairfield, Iowa's Dan Glenn (118 pounds) won his first of three Big Ten titles and New York's Steve Hunte (134 pounds) won his second. Rapid City, South Dakota's freshman Randy Lewis (126 pounds) won on his first appearance at the Big Tens, and Greg Stevens (177 pounds), a name from the past, made his mark again by standing atop the Big Tens. Add two more names to this list at the NCAAs: Bruce Kinseth (150 pounds) finished second, and Scott Trizzino (142 pounds) finished third.

In **1979** we won our sixth straight Big Ten championship, which was held in Iowa City. I sat in the stands to watch the finals in an effort to take the pressure off the wrestlers. Five of our wrestlers made it to the NCAA finals, with Lewis at 126 pounds and Kinseth at 150 pounds, winning titles. Kinseth also earned the most pins in the least amount of time and the Outstanding Wrestler award. Others who made it to the finals were Scott Trizzino (142 pounds), Mike DeAnna (167 pounds), and Bud Palmer (177 pounds). Dan Glenn (118 pounds) finished third.

We had four Big Ten champions in 1980: freshman Ed Banach, Dan Glenn, Randy Lewis, and Lennie Zalesky. We were heading toward domination but didn't know it yet. At nationals in Corvallis, Oregon, we dominated the competition with eight All-Americans, many of whom were at their first NCAAs: Doug Anderson (167 pounds), Ed Banach (177 pounds), King Mueller (150 pounds), Dean Phinney (HWT), and Lennie Zalesky (142 pounds). All-Americans with more experience were Mark "Sleeper" Stevenson (158 pounds), Dan Glenn (118 pounds), and Randy Lewis (134 pounds). Upon returning home with our third straight and fifth, out of six, NCAA championship, we had our biggest local greeting and celebration yet. Basketball coach Lute Olson took his group of Hawkeyes to the Final Four that same weekend, so we celebrated together.

The 1981 season was a strong one, with seven Big Ten champions this year. Mike DeAnna captured his fourth Big Ten title, but he wasn't the only one winning titles. Barry Davis (118 pounds), a freshman, also ended up with four Big Ten titles by the time he graduated; Pete Bush (190 pounds), Lennie Zalesky (142 pounds), Randy Lewis (who was injured this year), and Jim Zalesky (158 pounds) ended up with three each; and Lou Banach (HWT) and Scott Trizzino (150 pounds) each won two. Tim Riley (126 pounds) only ended up winning one Big Ten title, but ended as a three-time All-American. So this 1981 Big Ten team ended up holding a total of twenty-six Big Ten titles. That's impressive, but they really peaked at the NCAAs, where we had nine All-Americans. Five wrestlers made it to the finals, with only two champions—Ed and Lou Banach—but the team won convincingly.

We had a big win at the Big Tens in 1982 with seven champions. Jeff Kerber won his first of three Big Ten titles. Nationals were in Ames, Iowa, and we ended up with eight All-Americans, three of whom won gold:

Barry Davis (118 pounds), Jim Zalesky (158 pounds), and Pete Bush (190 pounds). We had two other finalists, Ed Banach (177 pounds) and Lennie Zalesky (142 pounds), who were very capable, of course, but they had strong opponents in Oklahoma's Mark Schultz and Andre Metzger. Lou Banach (HWT) had an injury-plagued season but ended up placing third when he pinned a 400-plus-pound wrestler named Tab Thacker of North Carolina State. I'm not sure I had Lou for one full practice this season, so his contribution was pretty phenomenal. Jeff Kerber (134 pounds) and Dave Fitzgerald (167 pounds) both made All-American.

Carver-Hawkeye Arena opened in January of 1983, and the Big Tens were held there. We had nine champions, which was a record performance. Jeff Kerber pulled out an amazing win by faking an over-hook hand drive and hitting a lateral drop off his opponent's reaction in a big scoring move to pull out his final match. Rico Chiapparelli (167 pounds), a first-year freshman, was the only nonwinner, but he still qualified for the NCAAs in Oklahoma, where he contributed to our big team victory. We had nine All-Americans and four national champions: Ed Banach (190 pounds), Lou Banach (HWT), Barry Davis (126 pounds), and Jim Zalesky (158 pounds). Duane Goldman (177 pounds) finished second, Harlan Kistler (142 pounds) finished third, Jim Heffernan (150 pounds) finished fourth, and Tim Riley (118 pounds) finished fifth.

In 1984 we had seven Big Ten champions, with Pete Bush (190 pounds), Jim Zalesky (158 pounds), and Jeff Kerber (142 pounds) each getting their third. Two new Kistlers, Lindley (167 pounds) and Marty (150 pounds), took over for their brother Harlan. Duane Goldman (177 pounds) won his second of four conference titles, and newcomer Greg Randall (134 pounds) started strong with a title of his own. We had five finalists at the NCAAs: Jim Zalesky, Duane Goldman, Lindley and Marty Kistler, and Greg Randall. Only Jim Zalesky ended up winning his final match, and his performance also brought home the Outstanding Wrestler award. I'm sure he would have given that trophy up for the others to win their own final matches as well though.

We had eight Big Ten champions in 1985, with first-time winners Rico Chiapparelli (177 pounds), Kevin Dresser (142 pounds), and Matt Egeland (118 pounds). Barry Davis (126 pounds), Duane Goldman (190 pounds),

Jim Heffernan (150 pounds), and both Kistlers, Marty at 158 pounds and Lindley at 167 pounds, added to their Big Ten title count. Five wrestlers made it to the NCAA finals, led by victors Barry Davis and Marty Kistler. Matt Egeland, Duane Goldman, and Jim Heffernan each finished in second place. Kevin Dresser, in his first appearance at the NCAAs, finished fourth. Lindley Kistler, Rico, and Randall all ended in fifth place. We ended up with nine All-Americans, and a huge win with 145.25 points to runner-up Oklahoma's 98.5 points.

The year **1986** was difficult off the mat with this team, though the winning continued on the mat. We ended with seven Big Ten champions, with Royce Alger (158 pounds) and Brad Penrith (126 pounds) winning their first Big Ten titles. Brad had not been the official starter until the Big Tens, where he replaced another nationally ranked first-timer, Paul Glynn, and ended up winning the Big Ten's Wrestler of the Year. Rico Chiapparelli and Kevin Dresser each won their second Big Ten titles, Jim Heffernan and Marty Kistler each tucked away their third, and Duane Goldman got his fourth. At the NCAAs we had eight All-Americans, and five NCAA champions: Penrith, Dresser, Heffernan, Marty Kistler (now at 167 pounds), and Goldman. This was Goldman's fourth and final try for an NCAA title after placing second the three previous seasons. Randall's second-place finish was our only loss in the finals, but even having six finalists was quite a feat. Rico's fourth-place finish moved him up one notch from the year before. Royce did not have his best performance and ended up in fifth place. I'm sure the pain of those losses helped drive him to win the next two NCAA titles.

In **1987** we were going for our tenth consecutive NCAA team championship, the all-time record for any sport. But we were too out of control and acting and thinking like this would just happen automatically. The leader (me) did not make the proper decisions regarding discipline and work ethic. We had six Big Ten champions this year, but we hadn't had any less than seven since 1980. Four were returning Big Ten champions: Royce Alger (167 pounds), Rico Chiapparelli (177 pounds), Jim Heffernan (150 pounds), and Brad Penrith (126 pounds). Two new Big Ten champions were footballer Mark Sindlinger (HWT) and Johnny Regan (118 pounds). At the NCAAs, we only had six All-Americans, the lowest number since

1979. Royce and Rico finished as champions, Jim Heffernan and Brad Penrith took second, and Mark Sindlinger was fourth. John Heffernan finished sixth at 158 pounds and scored valuable points for the Hawks. The Hawkeyes ended up taking second place to Iowa State and Coach Jim Gibbons. The NCAA championship streak that began with a half-point victory in 1978 over Iowa State came to an end in 1987 with the Hawkeyes finishing second to Iowa State. Same venue. Same team. The streak started and ended with my alma mater. It was only fitting, I suppose.

The years 1988, 1989, and 1990 were lean compared to the previous decade plus. We had four Big Ten champions in **1988**: Royce Alger (177 pounds), John Heffernan (158 pounds), Brad Penrith (126 pounds), and Mark Sindlinger (HWT). There were five All-Americans at the NCAAs: Sindlinger, Heffernan, and our three finalists, Joe Melchiore (who took second at 134 pounds), Brad Penrith (second place), and Royce Alger (first place). There were some really good things going on this year, with kids making sacrifices for the team. Royce moved all the way up to 177 pounds to help the team. Brad cleaned up his life for the better and almost won the NCAA tournament, losing 5–4 to Penn State's Jim Martin in the finals. With Tom and Terry Brands and Mark Reiland redshirting this year, we were building future firepower. The comeback was obvious, but most people couldn't see it yet, including me. We took second place as a team for the second year in a row, this time to Bobby Douglas's Arizona State team in their only NCAA wrestling championship.

The year **1989** was humbling. We had only one Big Ten champion, Tom Brands at 126 pounds, who was named Outstanding Wrestler of the tournament. We had four All-Americans at the NCAAs: Steve Martin (118 pounds), Tom Brands (126 pounds), Joe Melchiore (134 pounds), and Mark Reiland (158 pounds). We worked our way into title contention but fell short at the end to finish in sixth place as a team, the lowest finish in my history as head coach. We ended up with no team trophy, no finalists, and lots of work to do. After this NCAA tournament, I handwrote the Year-Round Plan, which was designed to put us back on top. Our younger wrestlers were firing up our close followers though, and two more young recruits in the room, the identical twins Troy and Terry Steiner, further added to the vision.

We only had two Big Ten champions in **1990**, Terry Brands (126 pounds) and Brooks Simpson (190 pounds), but we were back up to six All-Americans and three wrestlers in the finals at the NCAA tournament. Both Brands brothers took first place (Tom now at 134 pounds), Simpson took second, Bart Chelesvig (167 pounds) took third, Troy Steiner (142 pounds) got fifth, and Doug Streicher (150 pounds) got sixth. The team came in third place, so we were moving back up. With Simpson being the only senior, and the rest freshmen and sophomores, the stage was set for another move forward.

In 1991 we moved up to having five Big Ten champions, none of whom were seniors. Both Brandses got a Big Ten title this year, as did Syracuse University transfer Tom Ryan, who walked on at 158 pounds, and newcomer Chad Zaputil (118 pounds). Troy Steiner (142 pounds) also won his first of three Big Ten titles. Two weeks later at the NCAA tournament in Iowa City, we were back up to par with nine All-Americans. Only two of our six finalists won: Tom Brands (134 pounds) and Mark Reiland (167 pounds), who brought down the house with his final pin. This was a highlight after back-to-back losses for Zaputil and Terry Brands, then Tom Brands's win, and then Troy Steiner's and Tom Ryan's losses in their finals matches. Ryan's loss was heartbreaking, as he led most of the match until the last few seconds in a hard-fought match against Pat Smith of Oklahoma State. I worked extremely hard from the corner during that match, and it was difficult to walk out of the arena without passing out afterward. The next match gave both the crowd and me much-needed life with Reiland's big move and final pin. Bart Chelesvig (177 pounds), Travis Fiser (190 pounds), and Terry Steiner (150 pounds) all made All-American status as well. We won the NCAA team title for the first time since 1986. We were officially back on track.

The year 1992 saw us win six Big Ten championships, with both Brandses (126 and 134 pounds), John Oostendorp (HWT), Tom Ryan (158 pounds), Troy Steiner (142 pounds), and Chad Zaputil (118 pounds) taking home titles. Our previous year's ten NCAA tournament representatives were all back, plus past All-American Doug Streicher (150 pounds), making a team of eleven All-Americans going in. We finished with three firsts (both Brandses and Troy Steiner), one second (Zaputil), two thirds (Ryan and Chelesvig), and both Travis Fiser (177 pounds) and "The Big O"

John Oostendorp finished fifth. We scored lots of points and celebrated another big championship.

I wrote an entire chapter in this book on the 1993 season and all the moves and changes we had to make. It was a trying year, but we still won both the Big Ten and the NCAA championships, with Penn State now in the Big Ten mix. It was easier said than done, but the whole team pulled together to make it happen.

The year 1994 was not perfect. Ray Brinzer (167 pounds) and Lincoln McIlravy (150 pounds) were our only Big Ten champions this year. I made a late move to our lineup, pulling freshman Joe Williams (158 pounds) out of redshirt in February. I knew we needed help, and I really thought he could win the NCAA tournament. Joe was unique in his talent, but sometimes I underestimated the competition. And there was plenty of competition out there. Even in a wrestleback in the NCAA tournament, his opponent was injured, so Joe took it easy on him. Right toward the end of the match, his opponent exploded, catching Joe completely off guard. Joe lost the match and finished in seventh place instead of a possible third. Another late move this year was Daryl Weber, our starter at 158 pounds before making room for Joe to move in. Daryl couldn't move down a weight class, for Lincoln was there, and he couldn't go up, as Ray was there. So, making the move entirely on his own, Daryl went down two weight classes to 142 pounds. This was determination and desire at its best: Daryl just snuck off to make this new weight, and made it. But the way he made it drained him, and it showed in his performance. He came through though, and made All-American, placing sixth. We ended up with six All-Americans, two of which were champs: Lincoln McIlravy and Joel Sharratt (190 pounds). Jeff McGinness (126 pounds) finished fifth, Daryl Weber finished sixth, and two seventh-place finishes from Mike Mena (118 pounds) and Joe Williams put us in second place as a team. Our NCAA championship streak was back at zero.

We got going again in 1995 with six Big Ten champions: Mike Mena (118 pounds), Jeff McGinness (126 pounds), newcomer Mark Ironside (134 pounds), Lincoln McIlravy (150 pounds), Ray Brinzer (177 pounds), and Joel Sharratt (190 pounds). Joel was a defending NCAA champion, but this was his first Big Ten title, which was a bit unusual: one normally wins a conference title, then the NCAA title. Nationals were in Iowa City this year, and we had nine All-Americans. McGinness came through in the finals, but Lincoln and Sharratt were upset in their final matches. The other All-Americans were Mena, Brinzer, Bill Zadick (142 pounds), Ironside, Daryl Weber (158 pounds), and Matt Nerem (167 pounds). The Hawks were back on top again as national champions, but the upsets of Lincoln and Sharratt made the celebration difficult.

In **1996**, we only had four Big Ten champions, but we still won the team title by more than sixty points over second-place Penn State. This was Mark Ironside's (134 pounds) second Big Ten title, and the first for Daryl Weber (167 pounds), Joe Williams (158 pounds), and Bill Zadick (142 pounds). At the NCAA tournament, we finished with seven All-Americans and three national champions in Williams, Weber, and Zadick. Ironside moved up a notch to finish third. Mike Mena (118 pounds) landed his third time on the podium. And newcomers Lee Fullhart (190 pounds) and Mike Uker (150 pounds) earned their first time on the podium. We won the team title again and going three for three in the finals definitely helped the celebration.

The year **1997** was my final season as head coach. It was a close-to-perfect way to finish my career. I will always remember and talk about that championship, and I know I'm not the only one! The chapter called "The Final Season" is the review of all the crazy fun.

Names in the Sport

There have been many influential people in my life over the course of my career. The following are some of the most successful wrestlers, coaches, and contributors that our sport has to offer whom I've been associated with or just admire and respect.

KURT ANGLE

1990 and 1992 NCAA wrestling champion at heavyweight for Clarion

1995 freestyle wrestling World champion at 220 pounds

1996 freestyle wrestling Olympic champion at 220 pounds

Kurt Angle is a very interesting guy. In college, he wrestled heavyweight even though he wasn't the biggest guy, but he won two NCAA titles. When he had a chance to wrestle at 220 pounds internationally, he came through every time. Kurt has pretty much accomplished it all by becoming a professional wrestler and an actor. He made up his mind to be great, and that's how he ended up.

ED, LOU, AND STEVE BANACH

Ed: 1984 freestyle wrestling Olympic champion at 198 pounds, 1980, 1981, and 1983 NCAA wrestling champion at 177 pounds and 190 pounds for Iowa

Lou: 1984 freestyle wrestling Olympic champion at 220 pounds, 1981 and 1983 NCAA wrestling champion at heavyweight for Iowa

Steve: Wrestled for Iowa before becoming a lieutenant colonel in the US Army

Ed, Lou, and Steve Banach accomplished remarkable things and still are, especially given where they came from. They set the bar high with their exciting wrestling. Their book *Uncommon Bonds* is very much worth reading to see how they achieved all that they did.

WAYNE BAUGHMAN

1964, 1968, and 1972 Greco-Roman wrestling Olympian at 198 pounds

Sixteen-time national champion in four different styles—

collegiate, freestyle, Greco-Roman, sambo

1976 freestyle wrestling Olympic team head coach

Wayne is a true leader, especially in his commitment to staying in the sport at the international level for an extended period as an athlete. His coaching at the Air Force Academy, along with international coaching of USA teams, has made his leadership even more prominent. His efforts continue today by writing books and articles about wrestling and training. Good leaders always find a way to continue contributing to what they love. For me, during my collegiate competitions and beyond, Wayne gave me the attention I needed to build my confidence for competing and winning.

BRUCE BAUMGARTNER

1982 NCAA wrestling champion at heavyweight for Indiana State

1984 and 1992 freestyle wrestling Olympic champion in the super heavyweight division

Thirteen-time World and Olympic medalist

How Bruce settled into wrestling at the highest level for as long as he did — and won for as long as he did — is mind-boggling. Of course, being successful is motivating, and there are lots of good feelings that come with winning to keep you motivated. Also, USA Wrestling was now paying for the success, and that helped him to stay in the sport longer. There were also more wrestlers than just Bruce staying in the sport. Misery needs company in a tough sport like wrestling, but these guys were anything but in total misery, for lots of success means fun along the way, too.

DON BEHM

1968 freestyle wrestling Olympic silver medalist at 125.5 pounds

1969 and 1971 freestyle wrestling World silver medalist at 125.5 pounds

1969 and 1971 freestyle wrestling Pan-American champion at 125.5 pounds

1970 freestyle wrestling Tbilisi Tournament champion at 125.5 pounds

For me, Don Behm was pure inspiration, had great execution, and was a very good teammate.

JEFF BLATNICK

1984 Greco-Roman wrestling Olympic champion in the super heavyweight division

Former wrestling commentator for ESPN

Besides beating cancer, Blatnick followed Steve Fraser's hard-nosed style to gold at the 1984 Olympics. RIP.

DOUG BLUBAUGH

1957 NCAA wrestling champion at 157 pounds for Oklahoma State

1960 freestyle wrestling Olympic champion at 160.5 pounds

1971 freestyle wrestling World team head coach

At the 1971 NCAA wrestling championships at Auburn University, Doug approached me to work out. I had never really spent any time with him in this capacity before, but I agreed. We wrestled combatively for fifteen to twenty minutes with one or two breaks. Upon completion of our workout, he put his arm around me and said, "Gable, don't ever let anyone hint that you aren't an unbelievable wrestler. I've never had anybody do what you just did to me in that workout." I had to think about what I just did, as I wasn't that familiar with Doug's current reputation and the respect he had among his peers. My mentality grew from that conversation and workout. Doug coached me to gold medals at the Pan-American Games and the World championships later that year. Doug was the perfect person to coach me with my style of training and competing. RIP.

WAYNE BOYD

1969 NCAA wrestling champion at 123 pounds for Temple

Coach for Titan Mercury Wrestling Club

We can all contribute if we have a passion for this sport and for people. Wayne shows that, even though some may not think so. Part of coaching or being in charge is recognizing the value or the good in someone. There is plenty of good in Wayne, but sometimes it takes extra work to find it.

GLEN BRAND

1948 NCAA wrestling champion at 174 pounds for Iowa State

1948 freestyle wrestling Olympic champion at 174 pounds

I always measure people by what they do with their winning performance, and Glen put on a winning performance at Brand Hydraulics, the company he started with his wife in Omaha, Nebraska. Although he has passed away, he continues to be a big name in the sport, and he is the namesake of the Glen Brand Wrestling Hall of Fame of Iowa inside the National Wrestling Hall of Fame Dan Gable Museum in Waterloo, Iowa. RIP.

TOM AND TERRY BRANDS

> Tom: 1990, 1991, and 1992 NCAA wrestling champion at 134 pounds for Iowa, 1993 freestyle wrestling World champion at 136.5 pounds, 1996 freestyle wrestling Olympic champion at 136.5 pounds, 2006–present head wrestling coach for Iowa, winning three NCAA team titles

> Terry: 1990 and 1992 NCAA wrestling champion for Iowa at 126 pounds, 1993 and 1995 freestyle wrestling World champion at 125.5 pounds, 2000 freestyle wrestling Olympic bronze medalist at 127.75 pounds, 2008–present associate head wrestling coach for Iowa

One Brands brother would have been enough, but twice the punch produces knockouts. There was never a dull moment with these two, and their productivity is record-breaking.

JORDAN BURROUGHS

> 2009 and 2011 NCAA wrestling champion at 157 pounds and 165 pounds for Nebraska
> 2011, 2013, and 2015 freestyle wrestling World champion at 163 pounds
> 2012 freestyle wrestling Olympic champion at 163 pounds

It's too early to write in-depth about Jordan, for he is still in his twenties and wrestling at the world scene. He has already made his mark at the high end; now it's just how many more such marks he can make and for how long.

BOB BUZZARD

> Childhood friend from Waterloo, Iowa
> 1964 and 1965 wrestling All-American for Iowa State
> 1972 Greco-Roman wrestling Olympian at 149.5 pounds

At the beginning of my career, Bob Buzzard taught me more about wrestling than anybody else. His entire family was very helpful in building up my mentality and outlook on the sport, including his dad, Don Buzzard Sr. (RIP) and his younger brother, Don Jr. (RIP). Bob has put in a lifetime of wrestling work, and he's still at it.

CHRIS CAMPBELL

1976 and 1977 NCAA wrestling champion at 177 pounds for Iowa

1980 freestyle wrestling Olympian at 180.5 pounds

1981 freestyle wrestling World champion at 180.5 pounds

1990 freestyle wrestling World silver medalist at 198 pounds

1992 freestyle wrestling Olympic bronze medalist at 198 pounds

Chris was the most interesting wrestler I've ever coached from the standpoint of having very little wrestling experience and then taking it to the World level, retiring for nine years, and then coming back at age thirty-five and getting two more World and Olympic medals. How did that happen? If I had to answer that, I'd say that he was very disciplined in his lifestyle and that he was just one talented guy.

NATE CARR

1981, 1982, and 1983 NCAA wrestling champion at 150 pounds for
   Iowa State

1988 freestyle wrestling Olympic bronze medalist at 149.5 pounds

When I think of Nate Carr, I think of him launching his opponents like a missile. If he had let go of his opponents when he launched them, I'm sure they would still be orbiting the earth. You had to be careful not to get airborne with Nate. For anybody to beat Kenny Monday twice in the NCAA tournament finals—you're really good.

HENRY CEJUDO

2008 freestyle wrestling Olympic champion at 121 pounds

Henry Cejudo opted not to go to college right out of high school and went right into international wrestling instead. Going this route, he needed extra attention, and that attention came from one of my former wrestlers, Terry Brands. Being as young as he was when he won the Olympics, I don't know if he ever got as prepared as he could have been for another competition, and I think he needed that to continue wrestling. There was one major event that Henry Cejudo locked in on, and he won it. That event happened to be the 2008 Olympics.

KENDALL CROSS

1989 NCAA wrestling champion at 126 pounds for Oklahoma State

1992 freestyle wrestling Olympian at 125.5 pounds

1996 freestyle wrestling Olympic champion at 125.5 pounds

Kendall Cross has positively affected this sport through what he has accomplished. His story is great for kids, or for someone who needs to stay focused in any endeavor. Kendall is an example of someone who took on a challenge instead of taking an easier route, like moving out of a weight class where there was a two-time World champion in his way. He was not a favorite to make the 1996 Olympic team, so he had to do more work to make the team and win a gold medal at the Olympics, which he ultimately did.

KYLE DAKE

Four-time NCAA wrestling champion at four different weights for Cornell: 141 pounds in 2010, 149 pounds in 2011, 157 pounds in 2012, 165 pounds in 2013

Kyle is another unique wrestler. Nobody had ever won four NCAA titles at four different weight classes until Kyle Dake did it. His final athletic contributions are still to be determined, because he's still in the sport. To all the unknowns of the future: I'll be glad to make more comments on you when the time comes.

GENE DAVIS

1966 NCAA wrestling champion at 137 pounds for Oklahoma State

1972 freestyle wrestling Olympian at 136.5 pounds

1976 freestyle wrestling Olympic bronze medalist at 136.5 pounds

Gene was quite a competitor. He had all the ingredients of a World and Olympic champion. He stayed in the sport and walked away with a bronze medal at the Olympics. He's been a positive contributor to a lot of people in a lot of walks of life, including two of my favorite people, the Peterson brothers.

BOBBY DOUGLAS

1964 and 1968 freestyle wrestling Olympian

1966 freestyle wrestling World silver medalist at 138.5 pounds

1970 freestyle wrestling World bronze medalist at 149.5 pounds

1974–1992 head wrestling coach for Arizona State, including an
NCAA team title in 1988

1992 freestyle wrestling Olympic team head coach

1992–2006 head wrestling coach for Iowa State

Bobby Douglas is a guy who knows wrestling and the technicalities of the sport. He lived it, he breathed it—and he still does. He has been a huge contributor to the sport.

MIKE DUROE

1996, 2000, 2004, 2008, 2016 assistant coach on the Olympic wrestling team

2005 USA Wrestling freestyle coach of the year

This wrestler, coach, and friend has been around the world coaching wrestling for decades. He worked at the USA level in Colorado for several years, as well as coached at Cornell since the 2006 season. Other stops, including wrestling at Drake University, were in the UP of Michigan, Illinois, and Pennsylvania before Cornell. Mike has worked with the Hawkeye Wrestling Club throughout his career. We have caught a few fish together, as well as put on wrestling demos in many places. In the day, the combo of Mike and Doug Moses at camps resulted in very little sleep for them, but they always did great work for the youth!

STAN DZIEDZIC

1971 NCAA wrestling champion at 150 pounds for Slippery Rock

1976 freestyle wrestling Olympic bronze medalist at 163 pounds

1977 freestyle wrestling World champion at 163 pounds

Stan has been close to the sport for most of his life, and he is the current vice president of United World Wrestling. He made his living away from wrestling, but he used its principles when the going got tough. Stan has spent many hours on committees for the benefit of the sport, where many would have given up or failed. He led a tight, crucial battle that helped save Olympic wrestling. After the 1972 Olympics, I attended summer wrestling camps for kids for many years. Stan's home at the time was in East Lansing, Michigan, some eighty miles away. Around the summer of 1973, he just showed up at the camp and asked me if I would work out with him after the camp sessions. I couldn't refuse a good workout, so he basically drove ninety minutes each way, just to get his butt kicked for another ninety minutes. In reality, he got what he wanted and needed to help him become a World champion and Olympic medalist. He was a thinker and he analyzed details, so even though it was a long way to travel, Stan was laying the groundwork for his future performances. Stan is a smart guy and his plan worked. He came back to the camp every day when I was there.

BILL FARRELL

1969 and 1970 freestyle wrestling World team head coach

1972 freestyle wrestling Olympic team head coach

Bill Farrell was a late starter in the sport but loved the business of wrestling, coaching, and physical fitness. He brought ASICS into American wrestling, and it continues today with Nick Gallo and Neil Duncan. He seemed to love the drama and negotiations of competition in wrestling and in life. Bill figured out ways to get along with all kinds of people, especially in knowing how certain individuals could produce for the greater good. He adjusted to what was needed for individuals to create a total product, ending with very good, and often great, results. I have a lot of respect for Bill, and even though he has passed away, he is still carrying weight and building momentum for the sport. RIP.

FRED FOZZARD

1967 NCAA wrestling champion at 177 pounds for Oklahoma State

1969 freestyle wrestling World champion at 180.5 pounds

Fred Fozzard was a unique guy who adapted to the sport. He used a potential disadvantage to his advantage: he had polio in one of his arms, but he learned to adapt to make his wrestling even more effective. He never showed weakness in his wrestling, only strength. I trained with him at the 1970 World camp. Our conversations led me to be a more confident wrestler.

STEVE FRASER

1978 and 1980 wrestling All-American for Michigan

1984 Greco-Roman wrestling Olympic champion at 198 pounds

2007 head Greco-Roman wrestling national team coach for World
    team title
Brought home fifteen World medals throughout coaching career
Current chief of donor and alumni relations at USA Wrestling

Steve Fraser is the United States' first Greco-Roman Olympic champion. Those who recall his matches know that he earned his victories the hard way—by pummeling his opponents into the mat. He used his famous knockout headlock many times throughout his wrestling career. His job of dealing with resources for Greco is vital to Greco's future development and its success.

RULON GARDNER

2000 Greco-Roman wrestling Olympic champion at 286 pounds
2001 Greco-Roman wrestling World champion at 286 pounds
2004 Greco-Roman wrestling Olympic bronze medalist at 264 pounds

Rulon Gardner is a guy who made himself famous by winning a historic match over Alexander Karelin of Russia, a twelve-time World and Olympic champion. He then solidified his win with a World title. Gardner bounced back after multiple life-threatening injuries to win a bronze medal at the 2004 Olympics. He's a guy who would have died three times over if he didn't have the sport of wrestling. He survived because of the uniqueness of wrestling and what one has to master.

JIM GIBBONS

1981 NCAA wrestling champion at 134 pounds for Iowa State
1985–1992 head wrestling coach for Iowa State, including an NCAA
    team title in 1987
Commentator for the Big Ten Network, ESPN, and Iowa Public
    Television

Jim Gibbons is from an unbelievable wrestling family who has done a lot for our sport. I'm not so sure he should have beaten me in 1987. I think he lost some of his wrestling motivation when Iowa State stopped our NCAA championship streak. He wasn't in the sport that long as a coach, so it might be my fault for him getting out that early. We need good people like Jim to stay in long-term. We could have used more of his knowledge on the mat, instead of just on the mic.

JOE GONZALES

1980 NCAA wrestling champion at 118 pounds for Cal State–
Bakersfield

1984 freestyle wrestling Olympian at 114.5 pounds

The United States freestyle team was named the most successful team at
the 1984 Olympics. Joe was the only non-medalist in freestyle because of
an injury he sustained early in the tournament, which meant he had to
default out. Joe would have medaled if it wasn't for the injury. Joe gets
overlooked because of this, yet his close association to the sport has stayed
strong.

ADELINE GRAY

2012, 2014, and 2015 women's freestyle wrestling World champion

2016 women's freestyle wrestling Olympian

We have a great wrestler in Adeline, and she is also a great promoter for
women's wrestling. She is an advocate for our entire sport.

RUSS HELLICKSON

1971 freestyle wrestling World bronze medalist at 198 pounds

1976 freestyle wrestling Olympic silver medalist at 220 pounds

1979 freestyle wrestling World silver medalist at 220 pounds

1983–1986 head wrestling coach for Wisconsin

1986–2006 head wrestling coach for Ohio State

Russ is a funny guy whom I loved hanging out with. When many were
bashing the Hawkeyes for winning too much, Russ continued to try to beat
us. His ideal was to always move up, not bring the top level down. We had
a few intense coaching moments against each other over the years, but
they were for the good of the sport. He also taught me how to drink from
two soda bottles at the same time. (I decided to stick with one bottle at a
time.) Russ and I spent the summer of 1971 together at the Naval Academy
training camp for the Pan-American Games in Cali, Colombia, and the
World championships in Sofia, Bulgaria. Russ knew I wasn't normal when
we traveled home together after the Worlds. I got him to go for a good,
hard run and to wrestle in a park in Germany on our layover the day after
we medaled at the World championships.

SAMMIE HENSON

1993 and 1994 NCAA wrestling champion at 118 pounds for Clemson

1998 freestyle wrestling World champion at 119 pounds

2000 freestyle wrestling Olympic silver medalist at 119 pounds

2006 freestyle wrestling World bronze medalist at 121 pounds

2014–present head wrestling coach for West Virginia

Sammie Henson had the Iranians' attention when he told them they were the greatest fans in the world after he won the World championships in 1998 in Tehran, Iran. He wanted to make sure he could get back home. He upset one of my favorite Iowa wrestlers, Chad Zaputil, at the 1993 NCAA wrestling tournament.

DAN HODGE

1955, 1956, and 1957 NCAA wrestling champion at 177 pounds for
  Oklahoma

46–0 with 36 pins in college

1956 freestyle wrestling Olympic silver medalist

As a kid, I loved the stories of Dan crushing an apple with his bare hand, as well as smashing (pinning) his opponents. He's a great guy who has been great for the sport. I'm proud to be profiled alongside him in a book called *Two Guys Named Dan* by Mike Chapman.

KEVIN JACKSON

1991 and 1995 freestyle wrestling World champion at 180.5 pounds

1992 freestyle wrestling Olympic champion at 180.5 pounds

2009–2017 head wrestling coach for Iowa State

2018–present USA Wrestling national freestyle developmental coach

Kevin taught me something about coaching even though I was in my last few years as a coach at the time. It was during the 1994 World team training camp at Foxcatcher Farm. Not having coached a few of the athletes before, I should have eased in and won their respect before training them. Kevin was a World champion in 1991 and an Olympic champion in 1992, and he told me after the event that his goal was not to let me break him in practice. I learned an important lesson for the future in this: one step at a time leads to championship performances. This allows the athletes to focus on the proper goals. Kevin's goal should have been winning the

World championships in 1994, not me breaking him. We needed more communication and time.

MARK JOHNSON

> 1976 and 1977 NCAA wrestling tournament finalist at 177 pounds and Academic All-American for Michigan
>
> 1978–1990 assistant wrestling coach for Iowa
>
> 1980 national Greco-Roman wrestling champion and Olympian
>
> 1990–1992 head wrestling coach for Oregon State
>
> 1992–2009 head wrestling coach for Illinois
>
> CEO of YMCA Champaign, Illinois

Mark replaced J Robinson in Iowa's coaching staff to help keep the Hawkeyes on top of the wrestling world before moving on to his own top leadership. Mark and his wife, Linda, and family were so valuable in helping keep the Iowa wrestling dynasty intact.

TIM JOHNSON

> Commentator for ESPN and the Big Ten Network

Tim gives me credit for inspiring him, but Tim gives me inspiration. Not just through his lifestyle or his announcing, but also from the fact that he wrestled and that he had to wrestle with adversity. Tim never looked at his wrestling that way, but to battle through major trauma is pretty remarkable. Tim came through wrestling (like myself) with an extremely strong mentor in the high school ranks. Of course, mine was Bob Siddens, and Tim's, Bob Darrah. The rivalry and battles are historic.

ALLAN JONES

Allan, of Jones Management Services, has promoted and helped develop wrestling in his home city of Cleveland, Tennessee, and throughout the state. I have very much enjoyed and appreciated this continual support toward wrestling from Allan, his wife, Janie, and the entire family.

JIM JORDAN

> 1985 and 1986 NCAA wrestling champion at 134 pounds for Wisconsin
>
> 2007–present United States Congressman from Ohio

Jim beat one of my top wrestlers, Greg Randall, during the 1986 NCAA tournament finals. Even more impressive, he beat John Smith in the 1985 finals. I should be upset with Jordan for stopping me from going six for six at the 1986 NCAA tournament finals, but I'm overlooking perfection as long as he stays tough and smart in the United States Congress.

LLOYD KEASER

1971 and 1972 wrestling All-American for Navy

1973 freestyle wrestling World champion at 149.5 pounds

1976 freestyle wrestling Olympic silver medalist at 149.5 pounds

Lloyd Keaser did his best wrestling after college. He knew how to win tough matches, except for his gold medal match at the Olympics in 1976. That match was unique because he had split matches with his final opponent, Pavel Pinigin, each of which ended with no more than a one-point difference. Lloyd wasn't into it mentally before or during the match. It was a difficult moment because he could have won or lost that match by a regular decision and still won the gold.

JIM KEEN, MICHAEL DERGARABEDIAN, JIM RAVANNACK, RICH BENDER, MIKE MOYER, JOHN BARDIS, BILL GRAHAM, GREG HATCHER, JOHN GRAHAM, NOEL THOMPSON, BILLY BALDWIN, ANDY BARTH, MIKE NOVOGRATZ, JOSH HARRIS, ART MARTORI, DAVID AND KYRA BARRY, AND JAMIE DINAN

These are names that weren't mentioned every day in our sport until we lost our sport for six months in 2013. People such as these stepped up to help make a huge difference for the sport's future. Just to know that we have so many people out there who have these abilities and an interest in our sport gives wrestling a new outlook; they each stand out in their own unique way for their contributions. Several of the names listed above were already established heavily in the sport for many, many years, but in a crisis they always stand out even more. There are many more people out there whom wrestling still needs to cultivate. Many thanks to these individuals who stepped up!

LEE KEMP

1976, 1977, and 1978 NCAA wrestling champion at 158 pounds for Wisconsin

1978, 1979, and 1982 freestyle wrestling World champion at 163 pounds

1980 freestyle wrestling Olympian at 163 pounds

Lee Kemp made such an impact that he was able to leave the world of wrestling, go into another world, spend years in the car business, and then come back to the wrestling world as a coach and contributor. It shows the impact he had and that wrestling really never left him.

CARY KOLAT

1996 and 1997 NCAA wrestling champion at 134 and 142 pounds for Lock Haven

1997 freestyle wrestling World silver medalist at 138.75 pounds

1998 freestyle wrestling World bronze medalist at 138.75 pounds

2000 freestyle wrestling Olympian at 138.75 pounds

2014–present head wrestling coach for Campbell

Cary Kolat had all the tools physically to go to the highest level of wrestling. Because of politics though, the gold medals that should have been his went to someone else. In a normal situation, he gets gold medals. But in international wrestling, it was somewhat normal that he didn't get the gold. However, the number of occurrences went beyond the usual, even in international wrestling.

BILL KOLL

Undefeated in college

1946, 1947, and 1948 NCAA wrestling champion at 145 and 147.5 pounds for Iowa State Teachers College (now Northern Iowa) with an undefeated college record

1948 freestyle wrestling Olympian at 147.5 pounds

1952–1957, 1959–1964 head wrestling coach for Northern Iowa

1965–1979 head wrestling coach for Penn State

The word is that the illegal-slam rule was made because of Koll. I witnessed the "good old days" of his coaching when I went to one of his practices in the University of Northern Iowa wrestling room when I was in high school. Bill was there with a cigar in his mouth. Bill's family is carrying on his love of wrestling, and his son Rob is the current head wrestling coach for Cornell University. RIP.

RANDY LEWIS

1979 and 1980 NCAA wrestling champion at 126 and 134 pounds for
Iowa

1980 freestyle wrestling Olympian at 136.5 pounds

1984 freestyle wrestling Olympic champion at 136.5 pounds

Between Randy's throws and gut-wrenches, he dominated the Olympics.
There is much more on Randy throughout this book.

TERRY McCANN

1955 and 1956 NCAA wrestling champion at 115 pounds for Iowa

1960 freestyle wrestling Olympic champion at 125.5 pounds

Terry was a Hawkeye and an Olympic gold medalist, but he's best known
for creating many champions through the Mayor Daley Wrestling Club in
Chicago. People like Steve Combs, another former Hawkeye and Olympian,
and 1968 Olympic silver medalist Don Behm benefited from McCann's
legacy. RIP.

JIM MILLER

1974 and 1975 Division II NCAA wrestling champion at 134 pounds for
Northern Iowa

1991–2013 head wrestling coach for Wartburg, winning ten NCAA
team titles

Two-time Division I wrestling All-American

It's hard to believe that two Waterloo natives—one from West Waterloo
(me) and one from East Waterloo (Jim)—have amassed twenty-five combined NCAA team wrestling championships as coaches.

KENNY MONDAY

1984 NCAA wrestling champion at 150 pounds for Oklahoma State

1988 freestyle wrestling Olympic champion at 163 pounds

1989 freestyle wrestling World champion at 163 pounds

I've never seen anybody explode into a fireman's carry like Kenny. I know
wrestling pretty well, and when I see moves that are effective, I could pick
them up in my mind and execute them. I don't think I was ever able to execute Kenny Monday's fireman's carry. I've never seen anybody hit it like
him, and because of that, it makes him one of a kind. It's not the only one-

of-a-kind move I've seen him hit, either, and I've seen him hit those moves on some really good wrestlers in the world.

DOUG MOSES

1972 NAIA wrestling champion at 142 pounds for Adams State

1975 NAAU wrestling champion at 136.5 pounds

2005–present head wrestling coach for New Mexico Highlands

Doug is a lifetime wrestling friend, national champion wrestler, and wrestling coach. We go all the way back to junior high in Waterloo, Iowa. Doug is also a member of several halls of fame.

STEPHEN NEAL

1998 and 1999 NCAA wrestling champion at heavyweight for Cal State–Bakersfield

1999 freestyle wrestling World champion at 286 pounds

Ten-year career as an offensive lineman with the New England Patriots, including three Super Bowl rings

I really like Stephen Neal. One reason is because he showed that a good wrestler could perform in another high-end sport, like football, without a lot of training in that sport. His training was in wrestling, and he never played a down of college football. I always talk about being a wrestler and taking that into other areas in your life. Neal's attitude is what carried him to high levels in the NFL. His ability to score in wrestling and hold up in matches came through on the football field. He loves the sport and has helped a lot with building wrestling in California.

HAROLD NICHOLS

1939 NCAA wrestling champion at 145 pounds for Michigan

1954–1985 head wrestling coach for Iowa State, winning six NCAA team titles

Career college coaching record of 492–93–4

"Nick" created an atmosphere similar to my high school that just kept producing great wrestlers and great people. Coach Nichols's wrestling environment was based on giving the athletes independence. The wrestlers knew the structure was mostly dependent on them, instead of the coaches, so they had to have extreme discipline. He is a native of Cresco, Iowa, which is also the home of the Iowa Wrestling Hall of Fame. RIP.

JIM PECKHAM

1956 Greco-Roman wrestling Olympian at 174 pounds

1972 assistant wrestling coach for the freestyle Olympic team

Director of athletics for Emerson College for twenty-seven years

Jim fit in with anyone who showed a desire to work hard and be good. He loved the disciplined guys because he knew they were totally sincere, just like him. Jim told many stories of athletes becoming great, and they were all true stories that gathered many ears. RIP.

TOM PECKHAM

1965 and 1966 NCAA wrestling champion at 177 pounds for Iowa State

1968 placed fourth in freestyle wrestling at the Olympics

I've looked up to Tom my entire life. I think it's been good for both of us. Politics kept Tom off the podium in the 1968 Olympics.

BEN AND JOHN PETERSON

Ben: 1971 and 1972 NCAA wrestling champion at 190 pounds for Iowa State, 1972 freestyle wrestling Olympic champion at 198 pounds, 1973 freestyle wrestling World bronze medalist at 198 pounds, 1976 freestyle wrestling Olympic silver medalist at 198 pounds, 1980 freestyle wrestling Olympian at 198 pounds

John: 1972 freestyle wrestling Olympic silver medalist at 180.5 pounds, 1976 freestyle wrestling Olympic champion, 1978 freestyle wrestling World bronze medalist, 1979 freestyle wrestling World silver medalist

It's hard to believe what these two guys have accomplished in the sport, and how many lives they have touched. The book Ben wrote, *Road to Gold*, shows what we are capable of, even though we seldom know it ourselves. These brothers have influenced me a great deal, and without their influence, my commitments to wrestling and to my life off the mat would not have been as strong.

DAVE PRUZANSKY

6-time freestyle wrestling, Greco-Roman wrestling, and judo
Maccabiah Games champion

1971 freestyle wrestling Pan-American champion at 136.5 pounds

Current wrestling co-chairman for the Maccabiah Games

Dave is a former wrestling champion along with several brothers who helped wrestling shine and who still do. I stayed at his New Jersey home and vice versa for wrestling training back in the day. Dave definitely kept times lively.

ANDY REIN

1980 NCAA wrestling champion at 150 pounds for Wisconsin

1984 freestyle wrestling Olympic silver medalist at 149.5 pounds

1987–1993 head wrestling coach for Wisconsin

Andy was the victim of politics at the 1984 Olympics; otherwise, he would be an Olympic champion. The United States had dominated the freestyle wrestling competition, and toward the end of the competition there were orders to give breaks to the other countries. Andy Rein wrestled on the last day of freestyle wrestling, so the calls went against him. He realized this happens a lot in international wrestling, so he was not alone in this. He handled the entire situation very well. As the coach of the 1984 Olympic team, I didn't handle it as well as he did, so I'm still upset with myself. I could have helped more.

J ROBINSON

1970 and 1971 placed fourth and fifth in Greco-Roman wrestling World
championships at 180.5 pounds

1972 Greco-Roman wrestling Olympian at 180.5 pounds

1986–2016 head wrestling coach for Minnesota, including three NCAA
team titles

2001 coach for the only Division I wrestling team with ten All-
Americans

J helped me in my personal training, as well as helping the Hawkeyes to domination by being the main assistant coach for Iowa from 1977–84. We didn't always agree—but we were both right.

MYRON RODERICK

1954, 1955, and 1956 NCAA wrestling champion at 130 and 137 pounds
   for Oklahoma State

1956 freestyle wrestling Olympian

1957–1969 head wrestling coach for Oklahoma State, winning seven
   NCAA team titles

Considering that he coached for Oklahoma State, which was both Iowa
and Iowa State's biggest out-of-state rival, Myron was very influential in
bringing me along in freestyle wrestling right after college. He helped me
with finishing the sweep single and all finishes to explosion without hanging on too long. He put me up in his own home during a visit to Stillwater,
Oklahoma, for competitions in 1971 and 1972, and I worked at his camps
during the summer of 1973. At the finals of the 1972 Tbilisi tournament in
Georgia, the toughest tournament to win at the time, Myron pointed out
to me how much better I was since I had wrestled at the same tournament
the year before and placed second. It was just what I needed to win deci-
sively. As much as he was known for being a Cowboy, Myron saw the big
picture of the sport. RIP.

RICK SANDERS

1966 freestyle wrestling World bronze medalist at 114.5 pounds

1966 and 1967 NCAA wrestling champion at 115 pounds for Portland
   State

1967 freestyle wrestling World silver medalist at 114.5 pounds

1968 and 1972 freestyle wrestling Olympic silver medalist at 114.5 and
   125.5 pounds

1969 freestyle wrestling World champion at 114.5 pounds, our first
   World champion in wrestling for the United States

I loved Rick's entertaining style both on and off the mat. I only wish I
had had the opportunity to coach his mind to get him over a couple of
roadblocks for his future. He died shortly after the 1972 Munich Olympics,
where he won a silver medal. I'll never forget his small talk to me:

"Gable, you drink milk. Me? Beer!"

*"Gable, why do you talk about the Russians? It's the Japanese who
keep beating me."*

Sanders taught me how to cut the corner on a single leg, something I didn't do on him during our match in 1967, and I perfected the arm bars after being in a training camp with him in 1968 before the Mexico City Olympics. He also showed me his weight-cutting techniques, which were good since little work was needed while sweating a ton. Of course, education about nutrition and weight management is the rule today, but I personally enjoy his techniques. Most people won't get this, but I enjoy a great sweat. It's one of the times where my mind and body are feeling really great. RIP.

CAEL SANDERSON

1999, 2000, 2001, and 2002 NCAA wrestling champion for Iowa State at 184 and 197 pounds with a career college record of 159–0
2003 freestyle wrestling World silver medalist at 185 pounds
2004 freestyle wrestling Olympic champion at 185 pounds
2009–present head wrestling coach for Penn State, winning seven NCAA team titles

John Smith's low single-leg takedown started a revolution in scoring, but Cael refined it to the point of making this move almost impossible to stop. Cael is a lifer in the sport—teaching others and continuing to make a major impact. He is also the product of a very good family who has been involved in wrestling. It's pretty amazing that we were both Cyclones!

TRICIA SAUNDERS

1992 first American female World champion in wrestling
1992, 1996, 1998, and 1999 women's freestyle World champion at 101.25, 103.5, and 110 pounds
1993 women's freestyle wrestling World silver medalist at 103.5 pounds
Women's wrestling pioneer
First female inducted into the National Wrestling Hall of Fame as a Distinguished Member

With the future of wrestling depending a lot on the female wrestlers, I give a lot of credit to their early pioneers. Our most credentialed of that group is Tricia Saunders.

BILL AND JIM SCHERR

> Bill: 1984 NCAA wrestling champion at 190 pounds for Nebraska, 1985 freestyle wrestling World champion at 198 pounds, 1988 freestyle wrestling Olympic bronze medalist at 220 pounds, four-time medalist at the freestyle wrestling World championships
>
> Jim: 1984 NCAA champion at 177 pounds for Nebraska, three-time medalist at the freestyle wrestling World championships at 198 pounds, 1988 placed fifth in freestyle wrestling at the Olympics at 198 pounds

Bill and Jim emerged at the top of the sport through their outstanding performances, yet they are even better known for their leadership, especially in times that need great direction. Their ability to stay current and contribute at high levels is outstanding. We just need more of them. The Mobridge, South Dakota, natives attended wrestling camps in Mason City, Iowa, at North Iowa Area Community College in their younger years while I was headlining the camp. They also had early direction from our top international leader Stan Dziedzic—current vice president of United World Wrestling, the international governing body for wrestling. Jim was the executive director of USA Wrestling and the United States Olympic Committee. Bill was the chairman of the Committee to Preserve Olympic Wrestling when wrestling was dropped from the Olympics in 2013 and successfully brought back.

DAVE AND MARK SCHULTZ

> Dave: 1982 NCAA wrestling champion at 167 pounds for Oklahoma, 1983 freestyle wrestling World champion at 163 pounds, 1984 freestyle wrestling Olympic champion at 163 pounds, seven-time World/Olympic medalist
>
> Mark: 1981, 1982, and 1983 NCAA wrestling champion at 167 and 177 pounds for Oklahoma, 1984 freestyle wrestling Olympic champion at 180.5 pounds, 1985 and 1987 freestyle wrestling World champion at 180.5 pounds

I have to give credit to former Oklahoma head wrestling coach Stan Abel for coaching both Dave and his brother Mark. They were real characters who knew how to wrestle very well. I coached them on international teams, so Stan had them the majority of the time. They both were very respectful and actually did a few things they would not have done in their normal training because the team was participating when I was coaching them. The wrestling world was shocked and saddened with the murder of Dave by John du Pont at Foxcatcher Farm. But the Schultz name continues to carry promotional weight for the sport, as Dave's widow, Nancy, and Mark continue to support the wrestling world in positive ways. RIP, Dave.

JOE SEAY

1984–1991 head wrestling coach for Oklahoma State, winning two
    NCAA team titles

Joe Seay showed up out of nowhere and was one of the top guys I had to beat to make the 1972 Olympic team. He earned my respect from that. Today I think of him more as a coach than an individual athlete. He went from a Division II environment at Cal State–Bakersfield, where he won seven Division II NCAA championships, to a Division I environment at Oklahoma State and won two NCAA championships in a high-pressure environment. He did a great job of producing champions in the sport and bringing them to higher levels.

BOB SIDDENS

1950–1977 head wrestling coach for West Waterloo High School
Eleven-time high school state championship coach in Iowa
Long-time high school and college wrestling referee

Bob is still thriving and continues to draw a crowd. The impact this guy has had on people actually lasts forever. The impact he has had on me is off the charts. What a contributor to the sport! We need more coaches like him.

BRANDON SLAY

1997 and 1998 NCAA wrestling tournament finalist at 167 pounds for
    Pennsylvania
2000 freestyle wrestling Olympic champion at 167.5 pounds

Brandon Slay is a guy who took out one of the greatest wrestlers of all time, Buvaisar Saitiev from Russia, an eventual six-time World champion and three-time Olympic gold medalist. The two met in the opening round of the 2000 Olympics, and Slay was ready for him. Saitiev jumped into the match thinking it would be easy. When the going got tough though, Slay took it to him and upset one of the all-time greats. Saitiev wasn't able to adjust in the match against Slay. Saitiev could hardly stand up by the end, especially in overtime. Brandon is still a big-time contributor, and he's not letting up, having spent years working for USA Wrestling and now as the executive director for the Pennsylvania regional training center.

BILL SMITH

1949 and 1950 NCAA wrestling champion at 165 pounds for Northern Iowa

1952 freestyle wrestling Olympic champion at 160.5 pounds

Famous for "the whizzer," Bill pinned some great people with that power move. He's another great wrestler from Iowa. (RIP).

JOHN SMITH AND FAMILY

1987 and 1988 NCAA wrestling champion at 134 pounds for Oklahoma State

1987, 1989, 1990, and 1991 freestyle wrestling World champion at 136.5 pounds

1988 and 1992 freestyle wrestling Olympic champion at 136.5 pounds

1991–present head wrestling coach for Oklahoma State, winning five NCAA team titles

The Smith family (Lee Roy, John, Pat, and Mark) continues to make their mark in the sport of wrestling. John happens to be the one on top. His international accomplishments are so high (six World and Olympic titles in a row from 1987–92) that it will be extremely hard for an American to break his record of consecutive gold medals. John's nephews have made their wrestling marks, NCAA champions Mark Perry and Chris Perry. John's son Joe is wrestling now too, and time will tell his story. Lee Roy is the executive director of the National Wrestling Hall of Fame in Stillwater, Oklahoma, as well as winning an NCAA title in 1980 and a freestyle World silver medal in 1983. Pat was the first four-time NCAA champion, and Mark is a three-time All-American.

NAMES IN THE SPORT

TROY AND TERRY STEINER

Troy: 1992 NCAA wrestling champion at 142 pounds for Iowa

Terry: 1993 NCAA wrestling champion at 150 pounds for Iowa

Troy and Terry Steiner were put in lead roles to get Iowa back on top. Nothing has changed for either of them: Troy is currently the head wrestling coach for Fresno State, and Terry is the head coach for the women's national team for USA Wrestling, both positions holding a lot of weight for the future of our sport. The Hawks counted on them for their resurgence, and the sport is looking to them in a similar way now. You can count on them coming through.

CHRIS TAYLOR

1972 freestyle wrestling Olympic bronze medalist at super heavyweight

1972 Greco-Roman wrestling Olympian at super heavyweight

1972 and 1973 NCAA wrestling champion at heavyweight for Iowa
State

I know my limits, especially when it comes to Chris Taylor, who weighed over four hundred pounds. Chris and I roomed together in the Soviet Union for the Tbilisi tournament in a small room, side by side. I woke up in the middle of the night to a crash in the room. I looked over and saw that his bed had crashed to the ground. At the tournament itself, a buzz came over the crowd when Chris Taylor walked onto the mat with the team for his warm-up. Americans are used to warming up on competition mats, but the foreigners warmed up behind closed doors, so the crowd's first opportunity to see Chris was when he entered. He did a forward somersault from a standing position, and the place went crazy for him. He couldn't make a move without the crowd gasping. Back home in Ames, nobody left an Iowa State meet before Chris Taylor wrestled. A lot of people came just to watch him, and they never left unsatisfied or not entertained. It was his actions and his size that drew people in, and in person they loved his conversations. A great guy! Yes, I wrestled Chris in practices. RIP.

YOJIRO UETAKE

1964, 1965, and 1966 NCAA wrestling champion at 130 pounds for
Oklahoma State

Undefeated in college

1964 and 1968 freestyle Olympic champion at 125.5 pounds for Japan "Yojo" was as good as they get. He only opened up in a match when he needed to or when he wanted to. Opponents wanted to keep him at bay, which was their only chance of winning. This never happened though, since Uetake never lost a match in college. As a coach, he wanted to beat me at the 1972 Olympics with one of his Japanese wrestlers, Kikuo Wada, though, of course, he failed. Watching Uetake is where I learned the coaching technique of cracking your athlete across the face to get their attention or to get them ready. One needs a signed contract to do that today.

JAKE VARNER

2009 and 2010 NCAA wrestling champion at 197 pounds for Iowa State

2011 freestyle wrestling World bronze medalist at 211 pounds

2012 freestyle wrestling Olympic champion at 211 pounds

Like Glen Brand, Ben Peterson, Kevin Jackson, Cael Sanderson, and myself, Jake Varner is the most recent Iowa State wrestler to earn an Olympic champion banner in Hilton Coliseum in Ames. Good company joined already good company.

BOBBY WEAVER

1979 freestyle wrestling World silver medalist at 105.5 pounds

1982 placed third at the NCAA wrestling tournament at 118 pounds for Lehigh

1984 freestyle wrestling Olympic champion at 105.5 pounds

I coined the phrase in coaching, "It's over," from watching Bobby and his ability to get a position called the arm turk. This position opened up off leg-tackle takedowns and from riding very quickly. "It's over" meant that it always led to the pin! It was a great series of wrestling maneuvers. Not many have taken the time to master it, but for those who did, "It's over."

BILL WEICK

1952 and 1955 NCAA wrestling champion at 157 pounds for Northern Iowa

1972, 1980, 1984, and 1988 freestyle wrestling Olympic team coaching staff

Bill is one of my favorites. I learned a lot of little tricks in wrestling from him. He was an entertaining guy who could handle anyone in a conversation. I almost always picked him to be included on the coaching staffs I was in charge of internationally. Bill Farrell felt the same way, and I carried that forward. Bill had been coaching for well over half a century. RIP.

WAYNE WELLS

> 1968 NCAA wrestling champion at 152 pounds for Oklahoma
>
> 1970 freestyle wrestling World champion at 163 pounds
>
> 1972 freestyle wrestling Olympic champion at 163 pounds

It took Wayne and me a while to get acquainted, because we were both men on missions. Wayne being from Oklahoma, a rival of Iowa, also made it difficult to form a connection. We had our battles in training camps together, but not as many as one would think. We both seemed to have our partners whom we would stick with to give us what was needed for workouts. After he won the 1970 World championships, an injury kept Wayne out of the 1971 Worlds. The coaches at the 1972 Olympic training camp monitored him closely to prevent further injuries. Wayne won the Olympic gold that year in a gutsy, tough final match against Adolf Seger of West Germany. If you gave anything less than the perfect front headlock against Wayne, he would hit you with his duck under. Give an inch to Wayne on his top bar nelson, and your shoulder would be injured, no matter how flexible you were. Wayne's leg attack finishes were unique as well, for you would simply end up on your butt. We get along great now!

JOE WILLIAMS

> 1996, 1997, and 1998 NCAA wrestling champion at 158 and 167 pounds for Iowa
>
> 2001 and 2005 freestyle wrestling World bronze medalist at 163 pounds and at 167 pounds
>
> 2004 freestyle wrestling Olympian at 167 pounds

Joe was one of the most natural wrestlers whom I ever coached. His only loss in high school was when he was called for an illegal slam after being way ahead in the match. Joe responded to coaching from the corner during important moments better than anyone I coached. Joe earned two bronze medals at the World championships. He didn't learn to respond to his other coaches at the World level as well as he learned to respond to his high school coach, Bill Weick, and me. If so, his medals would have been gold.

SHELBY WILSON

1958 and 1959 NCAA wrestling tournament finalist at 137 pounds for Oklahoma State

1960 freestyle wrestling Olympic champion at 147.5 pounds

I loved Shelby Wilson. I didn't really know him until my competitive days in the early 1970s. Through Doug Blubaugh, Shelby helped out at training camps, and he reminded me of Jim Peckham's role at the 1972 Olympic training camp. He took care of the little things that people needed and always had a good answer to questions.

HENRY WITTENBERG

1948 freestyle wrestling Olympic champion at 191.5 pounds

1952 freestyle wrestling Olympic silver medalist at 191.5 pounds

In 1948, the year I was born, New York's Henry Wittenberg won a gold medal at the Olympics, and I bridged up on my head to get off my back while still an infant. The fact that he's from New York City always made him larger than life in my mind. New York is a place that's finally evolving in wrestling through the help of several of the individuals named here and also through Beat the Streets, an organization that gets kids off the streets and onto the mats. RIP.

CHUCK YAGLA

1975 and 1976 NCAA wrestling champion at 150 pounds for Iowa

1976 named Outstanding Wrestler at the NCAA tournament, the first Iowa wrestler to win the award

1977–1982 assistant wrestling coach for Iowa

1980 freestyle wrestling Olympian at 149.5 pounds

Chuck could have been included in chapter 8 as the "most efficient," for what he did in wrestling skills was well known but couldn't be stopped. His seat belt was the most famous and efficient, but his standing switch and his ankle hook and cross-face ride and pin make him great in all positions, especially in the collegiate style!

BILL ZADICK

1996 NCAA wrestling champion at 142 pounds for Iowa

2006 freestyle wrestling World champion at 145.5 pounds

Freestyle national team coach for USA Wrestling

Bill Zadick can't help but think of wrestling twenty-four hours a day. He was born into that environment through his dad, Bob, and his mom, Toni. They gave Bill and his brother Mike, a World silver medalist in 2006, their full support, which is what is needed to succeed at a high level. Bill is currently in a powerful position to lead the United States to the highest levels it has ever been.

JIM ZALESKY

1982, 1983, and 1984 NCAA wrestling champion at 158 pounds for Iowa

1997–2006 head wrestling coach for Iowa, winning three NCAA team titles

2006–present head wrestling coach for Oregon State

Jim was really good in competition. He had an explosive offense and the necessary focus to keep his opponent on the defense. He made wrestling look easy sometimes—and we know it's not. He always seemed to be one step ahead of his opponent, whether it was on offense or defense. Jim was the best example of my saying, "I shoot, I score; you shoot, I score." He's another lifer in the sport, and I like that. His older brother Lennie and younger brother Larry wrestled under me at Iowa as well. Lennie was a three-time All-American and went on to be a high school coach in Palmer, Alaska, before moving up to coach collegiate wrestling for the University of California–Davis. Lennie is currently coaching for California Baptist University in Riverside, California.

Index